POLICY PAPERS

NUMBER 36

LIKE A PHOENIX FROM THE ASHES?
THE FUTURE OF IRAQI MILITARY POWER

MICHAEL EISENSTADT

THE WASHINGTON INSTITUTE FOR NEAR EAST POLICY
WASHINGTON, D.C.

Library of Congress Cataloging-in-Publication Data

Eisenstadt, Michael.
   Like A Phoenix From the Ashes?: The Future of Iraqi Military
Power/
Michael Eisenstadt.
    p. cm. — (Policy Papers ; no. 36)
    ISBN 0-944029-54-X:
    1. Iraq—Defenses I. Title: Like A Phoenix From the Ashes?:
The Future of Iraqi Military Power II. Series: Policy Papers (The
Washington Institute for Near East Policy) : no. 36.
  UA853. I75E367 1993
  355' .0330567—dc20   93-34927
             CIP

Cover design by Jill Indyk
Maps by Michael Eisenstadt and Joseph S. Bermudez Jr.

THE AUTHOR

Michael Eisenstadt is Military Affairs Fellow at The Washington Institute for Near East Policy and author of two Washington Institute Policy Papers: *Arming for Peace? Syria's Elusive Quest for "Strategic Parity"* (Washington, D.C.: The Washington Institute for Near East Policy, 1992) and *"The Sword of the Arabs:" Iraq's Strategic Weapons* (Washington, D.C.: The Washington Institute for Near East Policy, 1990). He served as an analyst with the United States Air Force Gulf War Air Power Survey, where he examined Iraqi strategy and planning prior to the Gulf War, and has published articles in *Jane's Intelligence Review, Special Warfare,* and elsewhere.

CONTENTS

ACKNOWLEDGMENTS

The author would like to thank the following people who generously gave their time and expertise to read earlier drafts of this paper or provide materials which were of great use in its preparation. In particular, I would like to thank Amatzia Baram and Ofra Bengio who provided particularly detailed comments concerning an earlier draft of this paper as well as a great deal of useful information concerning the structure of the regime and its leading personalities. In addition, I would like to offer my thanks to Patrick Clawson, John Hannah, Simon Henderson, Yehudah Mirsky, Laurie Mylroie, Ken Pollack, and several other people who prefer anonymity, for their insights and comments on earlier drafts of this paper, and Joe Bermudez for his assistance in producing the beautiful maps which grace the text.[1] Finally, but not least, I would like to thank research assistants Peter Belk and Becky Diamond for their cheer, enthusiasm, and patience in chasing down obscure and sometimes hard to find sources and citations, and for preparing the text for publication. Of course, all errors of fact and judgment that remain are the responsibility of the author.

---

[1] The author would also like to thank *Jane's Intelligence Review* for permission to reprint portions of an earlier work, Michael Eisenstadt, "The Iraqi Armed Forces: Two Years On," *Jane's Intelligence Review*, March 1993, pp. 121-127.

GLOSSARY

A A A	Antiaircraft Artillery
ADOC	Air Defense Operations Center
A F V	Armored Fighting Vehicle
APC	Armored Personnel Carrier
C3I	Command, Control, Communications, and Intelligence
CBU	Cluster Bomb Unit
CIA	Central Intelligence Agency
DoD	Department of Defense
EMIS	Electromagnetic Isotope Separation
FAE	Fuel-Air Explosive
HUMINT	Human Intelligence
ICM	Improved Conventional Munition
ICV	Infantry Combat Vehicle
IOC	Intercept Operations Center
ITV	Improved-TOW Vehicle
MEL	Mobile-Erector-Launcher
MoD	Ministry of Defense
NBC	Nuclear, Biological, and Chemical
SAM	Surface-to-Air Missile
SOC	Sector Operations Center
TEL	Transporter-Erector-Launcher
UN	United Nations
UNSCOM	United Nations Special Committee

ABBREVIATIONS OF SOURCES

ACT	Arms Control Today
AW&ST	Aviation Week & Space Technology
FBIS-NES	Foreign Broadcast Information Service Near East and Southwest Asia Daily Report
FBIS-SOV	Foreign Broadcast Information Service Soviet Union Daily Report
FT	The Financial Times
GWAPS	Gulf War Air Power Survey
IAEA	International Atomic Energy Agency
IDR	International Defense Review
INA	Iraqi News Agency
JDW	Jane's Defense Weekly
JIR	Jane's Intelligence Review
JPRS-TND	Joint Publication Research Service Nuclear Proliferation Report
JPRS-UMA	Joint Publication Research Service Soviet Military Affairs Report
LAT	The Los Angeles Times
MECS	Middle East Contemporary Survey
MEDNEWS	Middle East Defense News
MEED	Middle East Economic Digest
MEMB	Jaffee Center for Strategic Studies Middle East Military Balance
NYT	The New York Times
PI	Philadelphia Inquirer
ST	The Sunday Times (London)
UN	United Nations
UNSC	United Nations Security Council
USSBS	United States Strategic Bombing Survey
W P	The Washington Post
WSJ	The Wall Street Journal
W T	The Washington Times

PREFACE

This January will mark the third anniversary of Operation Desert Storm. That extraordinary military action has had a long and troubled aftermath. Saddam Hussein remains in power, UN inspection teams have not yet gotten to the bottom of Iraq's unconventional weapons programs, and the potential for future Iraqi weapons systems development and military ventures are ominously real.

The Clinton administration has set forth a goal of "dual containment" that aims to constrain the destabilizing ambitions of both Iran and Iraq. Saddam Hussein may well be tempted to challenge this policy and once again attempt to realize his regional ambitions. Whether he will be able to do so will depend on the military capabilities at his disposal—and the resolve of the allied military coalition that forced his withdrawal from Kuwait, especially the United States.

In this exhaustively researched Policy Paper, Michael Eisenstadt, military affairs fellow at The Washington Institute, presents a comprehensive picture of Iraqi military capabilities past and present and provides a detailed analysis of how Saddam has gone about restoring the capabilities he lost during the Gulf War. This study yields valuable insights not only for U.S. Middle East policy, but also for the questions of proliferation and disarmament that have come to bedevil the world community in the aftermath of the Cold War.

Mike Stein
President

Barbi Weinberg
Chairman

EXECUTIVE SUMMARY

Despite its crushing defeat during the Gulf War, Iraq remains a potential regional power and the foremost long-term threat to U.S. interests in the Middle East. Iraq is still committed to acquiring nuclear weapons—it will continue to do so as long as President Saddam Hussein and his regime survive—and probably retains a residual biological and chemical warfare capability. Moreover, Iraq's armed forces are still the largest in the Gulf, and despite serious shortcomings, they pose a threat to Kurdish and Shi'i insurgents fighting in the north and south of the country as well as to neighboring Kuwait. Finally, Iraq has rebuilt much of its conventional military-industrial base since the war, as a first step toward its rearmament. For these reasons, Iraq is likely to be a major problem for the United States in the coming years.

Sanctions have thus far been extremely effective in preventing Baghdad from restoring its military capabilities, (as distinct from its military-industrial base), thereby denying it the means to once again threaten regional peace and stability. Their impact is manifest on several levels:

- The ban on the sale of oil (which could bring Iraq an estimated $12-15 billion a year in income) has been crucial in denying Iraq the funds that would enable it to once again engage in the large-scale smuggling of dual-use equipment and technology needed to produce nonconventional arms.

• The ban on arms transfers has prevented Iraq from restoring its conventional military capabilities by replacing its Gulf War losses, modernizing its aging inventory of arms, or acquiring repair parts for damaged equipment.

• The general atmosphere of hardship and privation in Iraq, caused in part by sanctions, has contributed to the widespread demoralization of the armed forces; this is a major constraint on its military freedom of action.

Moreover, UN weapons inspections have been key to uncovering Iraq's nuclear, biological, chemical, and missile programs and in achieving what coalition airpower alone could not accomplish—the dismantling of its nonconventional arsenal. Experience in the past two years, however, has underscored that while on-site inspections are likely to complicate efforts by Iraq to revive its nonconventional weapons programs, they are unlikely to succeed in detecting or disrupting all prohibited activities.

If sanctions and inspections were to cease, Iraq could rebuild its nonconventional capabilities in less time, with a smaller investment of resources, personnel, and money than it would take to restore its conventional capabilities. Iraq could probably produce nuclear weapons within five to seven years (much sooner if it were to acquire fissile material from abroad), restore its former chemical weapons production capability in less than one year, and produce militarily significant quantities of biological weapons within weeks (if it cannot already do so); this could cost a few million to a few billion dollars, depending on the nature and scope of the effort. By contrast, it could take five to eight years and many billions of dollars to restore its conventional capabilities.

Iraq's abiding interest in acquiring nonconventional weapons remains one of the most critical challenges facing the United States in the Middle East in the coming years. Iraqi statements and actions leave little doubt that the regime remains committed to acquiring a nuclear capability. Iraq has tried to preserve surviving components of its nuclear weapons program; it possesses a cadre of skilled and experienced personnel with the know-how to make nuclear weapons, as well as dual-use equipment which could be used to build them. In addition, future Iraqi efforts to acquire a nuclear capability will benefit from several factors:

- Iraq's nuclear program will be designed from the ground up to escape detection and survive air or missile strikes through the use of dispersed and concealed facilities and elaborate security precautions.

- Iraq will bring to this effort a detailed understanding of how to exploit the limitations of the UN's monitoring and verification efforts, conceal its activities from foreign intelligence agencies, and minimize the effects of bombing on facilities and equipment.

- The collapse of the Soviet Union may provide Iraq with unprecedented opportunities to acquire fissile material (weapons grade uranium or plutonium) and expertise with which to produce nuclear weapons, despite sanctions and inspections.

Iraq also retains a residual biological and chemical warfare capability. It has the know-how to produce biological and chemical weapons and it is believed to have saved critical production equipment as well as seed stocks for producing biological agents. Iraq could probably produce biological agents at this time, despite sanctions and inspections, and given the opportunity it would almost certainly revive its chemical warfare program. It might also still have hidden stocks of biological and chemical agents produced before the Gulf War that it is saving for future contingencies.

Finally, Iraq may have a scores of al-Husayn missiles that could provide a long-range delivery capability for stocks of biological or chemical agents which it may still possess. It could also use terrorist surrogates to deliver these agents against enemy population centers with potentially devastating consequences. For this reason, Iraq's continued involvement in international terrorism and its residual biological and chemical warfare capabilities provide reason for ongoing concern.

Although the main threat from Iraq in the future will be in the unconventional realm, its armed forces are still the largest in the Gulf and, if revitalized, could once again emerge as a force for instability in the region. Iraq now has about 400,000 men under arms; its ground forces consist of six corps with about thirty divisions, 2,200 tanks, 2,500 APCs, and 1,650 artillery pieces, while its air force has about 300 combat aircraft. Its navy—for all intents and purposes—no longer exists.

After the Gulf War, the armed forces underwent a major reorganization. The main elements of this reorganization include the reconstitution of the Republican Guard and the regular armored and mechanized divisions, the disbanding of large numbers of regular infantry divisions, and the dissolution of the popular militias. The net effect of these steps has been to strengthen the position of the regime *vis-à-vis* the regular military and the people, reducing the likelihood—at least in the near term—of a successful coup or uprising.

Although Iraq still has the largest armed forces in the region, it does not currently pose a threat to larger neighbors like Iran and Saudi Arabia since its armed forces continue to suffer from a number of critical shortcomings that inhibit its ability to engage in sustained combat, including: poor maintenance, severe deficiencies in the logistics system (particularly a shortage of wheeled transport), a lack of spares, and low morale. As long as sanctions remain in place, none of these problems is likely to be rectified.

On the other hand, Iraq could invade Kuwait or attempt to retake the Kurdish enclave in the north of the country. For now, however, neither of these steps is likely; Baghdad remains deterred by the prospect of U.S. military intervention, and by the difficulties its forces would face in undertaking even such limited operations. Iraq, however, remains a potential regional troublemaker since—as recent events have shown—it could draw U.S. air forces into combat if it were to once again challenge the northern or southern no-fly zones or sponsor acts of terror.

Finally, Iraq has devoted substantial resources to rebuilding its heavily damaged military-industrial infrastructure. It has reportedly resumed assembly of T-72 tanks (from unassembled kits acquired before the war) and limited production of artillery, short-range missiles and rockets, ammunition, small arms, and spares. Production remains far below pre-war levels, however, and is likely to remain so as long as sanctions continue to restrict its access to raw materials and spare parts for damaged machinery.

Iraq will constitute a potential threat to U.S. interests and allies as long as Saddam Hussein and his regime remain in power. Consequently, U.S. policy should actively seek the overthrow of Saddam Hussein and his regime, while aiming to contain Iraq by:

• Maintaining sanctions in order to deny Iraq the means to rebuild its military capabilities, and thereby undercut its ability to threaten regional peace and stability.

• Retaining a military presence in the region to deter Iraq and underscore the U.S. commitment to defend Kuwait and the Kurdish enclave against aggression.

• Maintaining the Gulf War coalition in order to preserve the viability of the military option in the Gulf and ensure the continued effectiveness of sanctions.

Because Iraq has traditionally played a role in both the Persian Gulf and Arab-Israeli arenas, the costs of failing to prevent its rearming are potentially very high. At stake are regional peace and stability, the Arab-Israeli peace process, the security of Persian Gulf oil, the future of regional arms control, and the achievements of the Gulf War—won at great expense and risk. For these reasons, the containment of Iraq—through deterrence and sanctions—must remain a cornerstone of U.S. policy toward the region for as long as the current regime remains in power.

INTRODUCTION

Despite its crushing defeat during the Gulf War, Iraq remains a potential regional power and the foremost long-term threat to U.S. interests in the Middle East. Iraq is still committed to acquiring nuclear weapons—it will continue to do so as long as President Saddam Hussein and his regime survive—and probably retains a residual biological and chemical warfare capability. Moreover, Iraq's armed forces are still the largest in the Gulf, and despite serious shortcomings, they pose a threat to Kurdish and Shi'i insurgents fighting in the north and south of the country as well as to neighboring Kuwait. Finally, Iraq has rebuilt much of its conventional military-industrial base, as a first step toward its rearmament. For these reasons, an accurate understanding of the impact of the Gulf War and international sanctions on Iraq's military capabilities is critical in analyzing the regional military balance, assessing the prospects for the regime, and identifying the challenges that lie ahead for U.S. policy in the region.

SADDAM'S STRATEGY FOR SURVIVAL

Since the Gulf War, Saddam has pursued three closely related goals: 1) assuring his own survival while reconsolidating his regime after the dual shocks of the war and the subsequent uprising; 2) restoring Iraq's territorial integrity, sovereignty, and independence while reducing foreign interference in its internal affairs; and 3) rebuilding the country's armed forces and restoring its capabilities (which is critical to achieving the first two goals).[1] In addition, Saddam has pursued a number of subordinate objectives:

• Seeking increased freedom of maneuver by wearing down the resolve of the United States and the international community through grudging acquiescence to UN resolutions when necessary, and non-compliance when possible.[2]

• Rebuilding Iraq's civil and military-industrial infrastructure as a first step toward its rearmament, and to underscore the regime's success at eradicating the scars of war.

• Eroding sanctions and ending Iraq's political and economic isolation by splitting the coalition through economic inducements, nationalistic, religious, and humanitarian appeals, and by portraying Iraq as a potential bulwark against Iran.[3]

• Salvaging Iraq's surviving nonconventional weapons production capabilities by attempting to obstruct the activities of UN weapons inspectors, while avoiding major confrontations.

• Blockading the Kurdish enclave in northern Iraq in the hope that political isolation, military intimidation, and economic hardship and privation will force the Kurdish leadership to seek terms with Baghdad, thereby breaking the back of the opposition.

• Undermining the Shi'i resistance in southern Iraq by destroying the economy of the marsh Arabs, who provide

---

[1] Phebe Marr, "Iraq: Rising from the Ashes of War and Rebellion," unpublished paper, p. 3.

[2] Marr, *ibid.*, p. 3. According to Vice President Taha Yassin Ramadan, Iraq "regard[s] all UN Security Council resolutions as unfair and unjust" and its compliance with them is a result of "certain considerations connected with the current circumstances" and "not...out of conviction." *Al-Sha'b*, January 26, 1993, p. 3, in *FBIS-NES*, February 1, 1993, p. 27.

[3] Marr, *ibid.*, pp. 3-4.

the insurgents with food and shelter, and desiccating the marshes which provide them refuge from the army.

Finally, Saddam will continue to seek revenge against the United States and its other enemies for Iraq's defeat during the Gulf War, in order to burnish the domestic and regional standing of his regime and to salve his own bruised ego.

BEYOND SURVIVAL: TOWARD THE FUTURE

Saddam's goals, however, are not limited to survival. He still entertains ambitions of making Iraq a regional power. This will hinge on Iraq's ability to rebuild its pre-war military might. Oil exports, which in the past accounted for about 95 percent of Iraq's foreign exchange earnings, will be vital to this effort, just as it was the main means of financing the pre-war military buildup. Iraq will not be able to sell significant quantities of oil, however, until sanctions are lifted.

The regime of sanctions now imposed on Iraq are set out in UN Resolution 687 and consists of three elements: 1) a ban on the "import of commodities and products" from Iraq (mainly oil—its most important export); according to paragraph twenty-two, the ban will be lifted following the dismantling of its nonconventional weapons programs; 2) a ban on the "sale or supply to Iraq of commodities or products"; and 3) a ban on the transfer of "arms and related material" to Iraq.[1] Thus far, sanctions have lasted far longer than expected and have been highly successful in preventing Iraq from rebuilding its military might.[2]

Saddam and his key advisors seem to believe, however, that because of Iraq's massive oil reserves (second in the world with more than 100 billion barrels), its value to the West as a large and lucrative market for its goods and services, and its potential value as a bulwark against Iran, sanctions will eventually be lifted. For instance, a recent Iraqi radio commentary claimed

---

[1] UN, S/RES/687 (1991), p. 7.

[2] Patrick Clawson, *How Has Saddam Hussein Survived? Economic Sanctions, 1990-1993* (Washington, D.C.: Institute for National Strategic Studies, 1993), p. 6.

that the embargo is "a problem for the whole world," because "as much as Iraq wants to sell oil to other countries and import from them," these countries want to "[buy] Iraqi oil and [export] their products to Iraq." The commentator also added that "the ability of these countries to manage without Iraq as an exporter and an importer is on a constant decline."[1] The fact that one of Iraq's top priorities after the war was to restore its prewar oil production capacity even though it is barred from selling its oil, indicates that it expects that sanctions will eventually be lifted.[2]

In addition, Iraq recently took a number of steps in meetings with UNSCOM officials in Baghdad in October 1993 which brought it closer to compliance with the provisions of Resolution 687 requiring the dismantling of its nonconventional weapons programs and thereby meeting UN terms for lifting the ban on oil exports. Specifically, Iraq provided data that it had long withheld concerning its biological weapon and ballistic missile programs and its foreign suppliers.[3] Iraq apparently hopes that the lifting of the ban on oil exports will be the first step toward lifting all remaining sanctions.[4]

If the ban on oil exports were lifted, Iraq could earn from $12-15 billion a year in income (after paying reparations mandated by Resolution 687 and reimbursing the UN for operating fees),[5] which would enable it to resume the large-scale smuggling of dual-use equipment and technology needed to produce nonconventional arms. Iraq would probably sell its oil at discount prices in order to create privileged trade

---

[1] Radio Baghdad, July 4, 1993, in *FBIS-NES*, July 7, 1993, p. 30. See also the comments by Information and Culture Minister Hamid Yusuf Hammadi in *AFP*, May 28, 1993, in *FBIS-NES*, May 28, 1993, p. 14.

[2] *MEED*, January 29, 1993, p. 21.

[3] *NYT*, October 9, 1993, p. A8.

[4] Iraq had previously asked the UN to authorize the one-time sale of $1.6 billion in oil authorized by resolutions 706 and 712, in order to purchase food and medicine. It stands to earn $934 million from these sales (the remainder being used to pay for reparations and UN operating costs). It appears to have abandoned these efforts, however, in the hope that sanctions will soon be lifted completely. *NYT*, October 7, 1993, p. A14.

[5] *NYT*, July 20, 1993, p. 1.

ties with key Western states and to carve out a niche for its product in a glutted market.[1] It has reportedly already held negotiations with oil companies from Britain, France, Germany, Italy, and Greece over oil exploration and marketing rights once sanctions are lifted.[2]

Lifting the ban on oil sales by Iraq might in turn cause countries like France and Russia—which stand to earn billions of dollars from business deals in Iraq—to press for the lifting of the general ban on exports to Iraq. With the ban on trade lifted, it would be very difficult to prevent the clandestine transfer of sensitive dual-use equipment or technology to Iraq,[3] or even to uphold the ban on arms transfers—since Iraq constitutes the biggest remaining untapped market for modern arms in the world today.

In addition, Iraq might seek to use the incentives of cheap oil and large development contracts to win allies in its effort to subvert the highly intrusive UN plan for ongoing monitoring and verification of its compliance with Resolutions 687 and 707 (which was approved as part of Resolution 715—which Iraq continues to reject) and is intended to prevent it from rebuilding its nonconventional arsenal.[4] If inspections were to cease, it could prove very difficult to prevent Iraq from rebuilding its nonconventional forces and from reemerging as a threat to regional peace and stability.

---

[1] Deputy Prime Minister Tariq Aziz has said that Iraq would probably sell its oil at below market prices since "even if we sell at $5 a barrel it will be a plus, since now we get nothing." *MEED*, July 16, 1993, p. 3.

[2] *WSJ*, January 29, 1993, p. A11.

[3] The UN's plan for ongoing monitoring and verification of Iraq's compliance with Resolutions 687 and 707 calls for the creation of a mechanism by which Iraq and its trade partners would provide advance notice of the sale or supply of dual-use items to Iraq. For details see: UN, S/22871/Rev.1 and UN, S/22872/Rev.1 and Corr.1. However, it is easy to see that this mechanism could be subverted by corrupt government officials and greedy businessmen who—persuaded by bribes or the prospects of large profits—will fail to report the sale of dual-use items as required.

[4] Laurie Mylroie, *Iraq: Options for U.S. Policy*, Policy Focus No. 21 (Washington, D.C.: The Washington Institute for Near East Policy, May 1993), p. 12.

This paper will review steps taken by President Saddam Hussein since the Gulf War to reconsolidate his rule, preserve what remains of his unconventional arsenal, reorganize the armed forces, and rebuild the country's military-industrial infrastructure, in order to assess Iraq's current and future military potential. In doing so, it will try to evaluate the efficacy of sanctions and UN weapons inspections in limiting Iraq's military capabilities, in order to determine the best way to contain Iraq, and to identify some of the main challenges facing U.S. policy in the future.

I SADDAM REASSERTS CONTROL: THE RECONSOLIDATION OF THE REGIME

The Gulf War (the so-called "Mother of all Battles") and the subsequent Kurdish and Shi'i uprising (the so-called "Chapter of Treason and Treachery") constituted the most serious challenge that Iraqi President Saddam Hussein and his regime—which is founded on the three pillars of the armed forces, the security and intelligence services, and the Ba'th party—have ever faced. The war left the armed forces defeated and in disarray while the uprising caught the security and intelligence services and the Ba'th by surprise; it was not clear at the time that the regime would prevail. In the end, the armed forces and the security and intelligence services crushed the uprising, while the Ba'th and its cadres—in a critical failure of nerve—simply melted away during the crisis.

These events produced major changes in the power structure of the regime. Saddam has come to rely on the armed forces and the security and intelligence services more than ever before to ensure his survival, while he has reduced his reliance on the Ba'th, traditionally the most important pillar of his rule. The manifestations of this new constellation of power are apparent on several levels.

• Saddam has lavished praise and honors upon the military for its performance during the Gulf War and the uprising in a number of highly publicized meetings and ceremonies. In the past military personnel were generally not recognized in public or given favorable treatment in the press due to Saddam's distrust of the military and his desire to prevent the emergence of rivals.[1]

• Saddam has publicly rebuked the Ba'th and its leadership, accusing them of losing touch with the people and losing sight of their primary mission—mobilizing the population in support of the regime. A key manifestation of the decline of the party and the rise of the military is the fact that at least nine of eighteen provincial governors are military officers. These positions were formerly the exclusive preserve of civilian party officials.[2]

• The rural tribes are being used by the regime to bolster its rule where its grip is weak, and they have been publicly lauded for their supportive role. In the past the Ba'th was the sole means used to mobilize the population while the tribes were officially portrayed as reactionary and backward elements. Historically, however, while the services of the tribes can be bought, their loyalty cannot, and it is therefore unlikely that the tribes offer a long-term solution to the problems caused by the current weakness of the regime.[3]

THE ARMED FORCES COMMAND

Following the Gulf War and the uprising, Saddam moved to reassert control over the armed forces and preempt potential opposition by replacing or reassigning his defense minister, chief of staff, and nearly every other general staff officer and corps commander, as well as large numbers of senior and mid-level officers.[4] This is in keeping with his traditional habit of rotating military personnel, so as to prevent military officers from acquiring too much influence and to eliminate potential opponents or disloyal elements. For instance:

---

[1] See, for instance: Ofra Bengio, "Iraq," in *Middle East Contemporary Survey* (N.Y.: Holmes & Meier), 1979-1980, p. 508 and passim: 1980-81, p. 585; 1983-84, p. 472; 1988, pp. 511-514; and 1989, p. 387.

[2] Amatzia Baram, "Is Saddam on His Way Out?" The Washington Institute for Near East Policy, PolicyWatch No. 57, October 29, 1992, p. 1.

[3] Baram, *ibid.*, pp. 1-2.

[4] See Appendix III.

- Defense Minister Gen. Sa'di Tu'mah 'Abbas was replaced in April 1991 by Minister of Industry and Military Industrialization Lt. Gen. Husayn Kamil Hasan al-Majid— Saddam's ambitious paternal cousin and son-in-law, and the man widely regarded as the number two in the regime.

- Husayn Kamil was in turn relieved in November 1991, stripped of all his responsibilities, and replaced by another cousin, Interior Minister Gen. 'Ali Hasan al-Majid, who led the brutal campaign against the Kurds in northern Iraq in 1988.[1]

- Chief-of-Staff Lt. Gen. Husayn Rashid Muhammad al-Tikriti was replaced in June 1991 by Lt. Gen. Iyad Futayyih Khalifah al-Rawi, the commander of the Republican Guard. Husayn Rashid was in turn appointed supervisor of the Republican Guard (a title previously held by Husayn Kamil), while Lt. Gen. Ibrahim 'Abd al-Sattar Muhammad was named its new commander.[2]

There have also been several reported purges of the armed forces since the war, although only two can be confirmed. The first followed the unsuccessful Republican Guard coup attempt in June 1992 which resulted in the execution or dismissal of nearly 150 mid-level Republican Guard officers.[3] The second purge occurred in August 1993 and involved the execution of six officers accused of involvement in a planned coup.[4]

THE SECURITY AND INTELLIGENCE SERVICES

Saddam has also reshuffled the heads of his security and intelligence services since the war. The security organizations

---

[1] Husayn Kamil has since been reinstated as minister of Industry and Military Industrialization.

[2] Husayn Rashid had previously commanded the Republican Guard in 1986-87. During this time he oversaw its dramatic expansion to a multi-division corps.

[3] *NYT*, July 5, 1992, p. A3; *NYT*, July 9, 1992, p. A3; *Newsweek*, July 20, 1992, p. 49.

[4] *PI*, October 10, 1993, p. A13.

are dedicated primarily to defending the regime and its key personnel, while the intelligence organizations have a broader role—foreign intelligence, internal security, the clandestine procurement of sensitive foreign technology, and terrorism. From the standpoint of the survival of the regime, the most important security organization is Special Security (*Jihaz al-Amn al-Khas*), which exercises operational control over two other key security organizations: the Special Republican Guard (*Al-Haras al-Jumhuri al-Khas*), and the Presidential Guard (*Jihaz al-Himaya al-Khas*).[1] Personnel in these organizations consist almost exclusively of Sunni Arabs from towns such as Tikrit, Dur, Sharqat, Baiji, Samarra, and Ramadi.[2]

- Special Security is headed by the president's younger son, Qusay. It is responsible for protecting the president, thwarting potential coups and other threats to the regime, and keeping tabs on the Republican Guard and the other security organizations. In the past it was also deeply involved in the clandestine procurement of foreign weapons and technology.[3]

- The Special Guard is the only heavily armed force permitted in Baghdad and is the premier praetorian unit in the armed forces. It is commanded by Maj. Gen. Kamal Mustafa al-Majid and consists of about 15,000 men who guard presidential palaces and other key facilities in the capital and

---

[1] Radio Baghdad, April 2, 1992, in *FBIS-NES*, April 6, 1992, pp. 23-24; Hussein Sumaida with Carole Jerome, *Circle of Fear: A Renegade's Journey From the Mossad to the Iraqi Secret Service* (Toronto: Stoddart, 1991), p. 217. In addition, another organization subordinate to Special Security—the Protective Strike Forces (*Quwat al-Himaya al-Iqtihamiya*) of Maj. Rukan Ruzuqi Sulayman al-Majid—is believed to have some kind of internal security function, although its precise role and its relationship to these other organizations is not clear. Laurie Mylroie, personal correspondence.

[2] Isam al-Khafaji, "State Terror and the Degradation of Politics in Iraq," *Middle East Report*, May-June 1992, pp. 17-19. These towns are located in the so-called Sunni Arab triangle, which encompasses the area between Baghdad, Mosul, and Ramadi.

[3] Special Security was originally established in the mid-1980s by Husayn Kamil. Simon Henderson, *Instant Empire: Saddam Hussein's Ambition for Iraq* (San Francisco: Mercury House, 1991), pp. 79, 88-89, 165.

elsewhere. The Special Guard was reportedly the unit that thwarted the June 1992 coup-attempt.[1]

• The Presidential Guard employs several thousand bodyguards and is headed by Brig. Gen. Arshad Yasin (a cousin and brother-in-law of the president), who is also his aide-de-camp, personal pilot, and foremost companion. Most of Saddam's bodyguards are from his home town of Tikrit and accompany him wherever he goes, securing meeting places and overnight sites for him.[2]

These security organizations are supplemented by three major intelligence organizations—General Intelligence (*Al-Mukhabarat al-'Amma*) headed by Maj. Gen. Sabir 'Abd al-'Aziz al-Duri,[3] General Security (*Al-Amn al-'Amm*) headed by Saddam's half-brother Siba'wi Ibrahim, and Military Intelligence (*Al-Istikhbarat al-'Askariya*) headed by Maj. Gen. Fanar Zibin Hasan al-Tikriti.[4] All three have, to some extent, overlapping foreign intelligence and internal security functions.

---

[1] *WP*, January 31, 1991, pp. A21, A23; Voice of the People of Kurdistan, February 2, 1992, in *FBIS-NES*, February 3, 1992, p. 24; *MEED*, July 17, 1992, p. 20; Laurie Mylroie, personal correspondence. The Special Republican Guard consists of units which trace their lineage to the original Republican Guard units. It was formed in the mid-1980s when the Republican Guard expanded dramatically to fulfill regular military duties. At this time, several units assigned to the traditional Republican Guard were redesignated as the Special Republican Guard, while the best and most loyal personnel were taken from regular army formations to form new Republican Guard units. Simon Henderson, personal correspondence.

[2] Sumaida, *op cit.*, pp. 217-218; *al-Majalla*, November 11, 1992, pp. 38-40, in *FBIS-NES*, December 9, 1992, pp. 28-31; Amatzia Baram and Ofra Bengio, personal correspondence.

[3] Real power in General Intelligence, however, reportedly rests in the hands of its deputy director, Col. 'Abd Hasan al-Majid, who is also 'Ali Hasan al-Majid's brother.

[4] During the Gulf War, Maj. Gen. Fanar al-Tikriti headed Special Security, Siba'wi Ibrahim was chief of General Intelligence, Maj. Gen. Sabir al-Duri headed Military Intelligence, and Maj. Gen. 'Abd al-Rahman Ahmad al-Duri headed General Security.

• General Intelligence, the target of the June 1993 U.S. cruise missile strike, is the largest and most diverse of these organizations. It performs both foreign intelligence and internal security functions and has organized terrorist attacks abroad, including the attempt on the life of President Bush during his visit to Kuwait in April 1993.

• Military Intelligence is responsible for collecting and assessing information about foreign military threats, keeping tabs on the military and monitoring disloyal elements in its ranks. It too has organized terrorist attacks abroad, including the 1982 attempt on the life of Israel's ambassador in London, Shlomo Argov.

• General Security, by contrast, has a narrower internal security role and is the primary organization fulfilling this function.

These organizations have often been headed by relatives of Saddam—and their chiefs report directly to Saddam or to his secretary, Brig. Gen. 'Abd Hamid Mahmud, who, because of his access to the president and his position, is one of the most powerful figures in the president's entourage.[1] In addition, while all three intelligence organizations are headquartered in Baghdad, General Intelligence and General Security operate numerous field offices in cities and towns throughout the country, enabling the regime to infiltrate nearly every corner of society. Similarly, Military Intelligence has representatives and informers throughout the military.

Saddam's success in surviving both the Gulf War and the subsequent turmoil was no small achievement. Saddam's survival demonstrated the extraordinary efficiency of his security and intelligence services, and the effectiveness of the measures taken to protect him against coups and assassinations—which proved equally successful in protecting him against coalition air strikes and the upheavals which followed the war.

---

[1] Laurie Mylroie, personal correspondence.

These measures, first of all, include hardened underground command bunkers and mobile command posts. Several of Saddam's palaces and military command posts are equipped with hardened underground bunkers fitted with NBC filtration systems and stocked with several months of provisions.[1] Saddam, however, reportedly avoided these sites during the war since he believed coalition forces would target them. Saddam also employed several mobile command posts (modified civilian recreational vehicles) to enable him to maintain command and control as he moved around the country.[2]

Moreover, Saddam's whereabouts and movements are cloaked in absolute secrecy, and are known only to a select circle of deputies. Official meetings are rarely held in government buildings or facilities, or command bunkers— usually they take place in inconspicuous locations such as private homes or apartments.[3] Saddam's bodyguards will usually secure several sites for a meeting or overnight stay, with Saddam selecting the one to be used at the last moment. In addition, Saddam rarely stays in one place for more than a few hours, and relies on false convoys and look-alikes to confuse potential assassins.[4]

Finally, Saddam's personal security is provided for by several competing organizations to reduce the possibility of his bodyguards being involved in a coup or assassination attempt. During public appearances, uniformed bodyguards from the Presidential Guard serve as Saddam's inner ring of protection,

---

[1] *Quick*, August 23-29, 1990, pp. 26-27; *Bunte*, January 17, 1991, pp. 24-27; *Bild*, January 24, 1991, p. 2; *Allgemeine Zeitung*, January 24, 1991, p. 1.

[2] General Sir Peter De La Billiere, *Storm Command: A Personal Account of the Gulf War* (London: HarperCollins, 1993), p. 260; *Newsday*, June 23, 1991, p. A16.

[3] For instance, in a February 1991 interview Soviet envoy Y. A. Primakov related that during a diplomatic mission to Iraq earlier that month, the Soviet delegation "met [Saddam] in an ordinary house, not a bunker. We had thought that this was a 'crossing point' and that we would be kept there a while and then taken to Saddam. But no, Saddam Husayn and the entire leadership came to us [there]." *Literaturnaya Gazeta*, February 27, 1991, p. 4, in *JPRS-UMA*, March 18, 1991, p. 27.

[4] *Al-Majalla*, *op cit.*, pp. 38-40; Amatzia Baram, personal correspondence.

although these are frequently rotated for security reasons. They are supplemented by uniformed and plainclothes personnel from General Intelligence and General Security who are responsible for general area security and crowd control.[1] Visitors are thoroughly screened and checked by security personnel prior to private audiences with Saddam, who usually wears a bulletproof vest and sidearm for his own protection.[2]

Iraq's security and intelligence organizations suffered a number of major blows during the war and in its aftermath. Nearly every intelligence headquarters building in Baghdad was bombed repeatedly during the war, and several regional intelligence headquarters were gutted during the uprising, their files ransacked or destroyed.[3] In addition, the closing of Iraqi diplomatic representations around the world prior to the war and the expulsion of its agents operating under diplomatic cover have hampered overseas activities. Nonetheless, Iraq's intelligence services have been very active since the war, indicating that they have largely recovered from these setbacks.

For instance, Iraqi intelligence continues to run agents in Kuwait, some of whom were involved in the aborted attempt on the life of President George Bush during his April 1993 visit there. Other activities since the war include: a terrorist campaign in Kurdistan targeting local officials and foreign aid workers in an effort to demoralize and isolate the Kurds; the murder in Amman in December 1992 of an expatriate Iraqi nuclear scientist; the dispatch of agents abroad to track opponents of the regime and report on their activities; and the

---

[1] Sumaida, *op cit.,* pp. 217-218.

[2] Former presidential bodyguard Maj. Karim 'Abdallah al-Juburi, in *al-Majalla,* January 9, 1991, pp. 14-15, 18, in *JPRS-NEA,* February 12, 1991, pp. 10-19; and *Le Nouvel Observateur,* December 20-26, 1990, pp. 34-39.

[3] General Intelligence headquarters was again struck by cruise missiles in June 1993, in retaliation for its role in the assassination attempt against President George Bush.

revival of clandestine overseas procurement networks to help Iraq circumvent sanctions.[1]

Iraq also continues to provide sanctuary and to maintain contacts with terrorist organizations and individuals who have served as Iraqi surrogates in the past, including the Abu Nidal Organization (ANO), the Arab Liberation Front (ALF), the Palestine Liberation Front (PLF) of Abu 'Abbas, and Abu Ibrahim—leader and master bombmaker of the defunct 15 May Organization. It thus retains the option of sponsoring terrorist acts by these groups should it desire to do so in the future. It likewise provides safehaven and military support for the Turkish Kurdistan Workers Party (PKK) and the Iranian Mojahedin-e Khalq Organization (MKO), which it has used as surrogates in its conflict with its two larger neighbors.[2]

CONCLUSIONS

The cumulative impact of actions taken since the war—the rotation of the armed forces' senior commanders and of the security and intelligence chiefs, and the reconsolidation of the regime's repressive apparatus—has been to effectively preclude the emergence of an organized opposition in the armed forces and the security and intelligence services, and any serious, broad-based popular challenge to the regime. There are, however, signs of fissures in Saddam's power base.

Specifically, there have been persistent reports of growing opposition to Saddam among fellow Tikritis—indicating that discontent has penetrated to the heart of the regime—as well as members of a number of important Sunni Arab and Shi'i tribes whose sons occupy key positions in the regime. Tikritis were reportedly involved in the planned August 1993 coup, while Saddam has dismissed members of the al-Jubur (a mixed Sunni-Shi'i tribe) who fill key positions in the military and in the security and intelligence services, because members of the tribe were involved in coup attempts in January 1989, August

---

[1] U.S. Department of State, *Patterns of Global Terrorism: 1992*, April 1993, pp. 22-23; *MEDNEWS*, September 28, 1992, pp. 2-3.
[2] U.S. Department of State, *ibid.*, pp. 22-23.

1991, and June 1992.[1] Personnel belonging to the Sunni Arab Dulaym and 'Ubayd have likewise reportedly been purged from the military as a result of the activities of some members of these tribes, although many continue to serve.

The erosion of support for Saddam among his wider circle of supporters has forced him to increasingly rely on members of his own extended family to fill vital positions in the regime. As a result, the social base of the regime has narrowed; this is a source of vulnerability which could eventually undermine the stability of the regime. On the other hand, because many of those who now surround Saddam are bound to him by ties of kinship or marriage, they are unlikely to turn against the regime since they benefit most from its survival and would share a common fate if it were to fall.

---

[1] *PI*, October 10, 1993, p. A13; *Le Nouvel Observateur*, December 20-26, 1990, pp. 34-39; *al-Majalla*, January 9, 1991, pp. 14-15, 18. See also the interview with Dr. Husayn Muhammad 'Abdallah al-Juburi, former professor at Mosul University, in *al-Wasat*, April 19, 1993, pp. 34-36, in *FBIS-NES*, April 23, 1993, pp. 34-37.

II   IRAQ'S NONCONVENTIONAL FORCES

Before the Gulf War, Iraq had the most advanced and ambitious nonconventional weapons program in the Arab world. It was developing nuclear, biological, and chemical weapons, as well as missiles and superguns to deliver them. However, coalition air strikes during the Gulf War and subsequent actions by UN weapons inspectors have succeeded in destroying most of Iraq's known nonconventional capabilities.

The authority for UN efforts to dismantle Iraq's nonconventional capabilities is derived from Resolutions 687, 707, and 715:

- Resolution 687 requires Iraq to dismantle its nuclear, biological, and chemical weapons and ballistic missile programs and links the lifting of the ban on oil sales to compliance with this aspect of the resolution.[1]

---

[1] Resolution 687, passed on April 3, 1991, requires Iraq to "accept the destruction, removal, or rendering harmless" of all nuclear, chemical, and biological weapons, "research, development, support or manufacturing facilities," "all chemical and biological weapons" and "stocks of agents," and "all ballistic missiles with a range greater than 150 kilometers," as well as related production and repair facilities. It also stipulates that "upon [Security Council] agreement that Iraq has completed all [these] actions" the "prohibitions against the import of commodities and products originating in Iraq...shall have no further force or effect." UN, S/RES/687 (1991), April 3, 1991.

- Resolution 707 requires Iraq to fully disclose all aspects of these programs and halt all nuclear activities except for the use of isotopes for medical, agricultural, or industrial purposes.[1]

- Resolution 715 requires Iraq to accept its obligations under the UN plan for the ongoing monitoring and verification of its compliance with Resolutions 687 and 707, which is to be accomplished through inspections, aerial overflights, and the provision of information by Iraq.[2]

To date, Iraq has repeatedly sought to obstruct efforts to dismantle its nonconventional weapons programs as provided for by Resolutions 687 and 707, and it continues to reject Resolution 715—which it claims would undermine its sovereignty and independence. The following is a survey of Iraq's nonconventional weapons programs before the war and an assessment of its current and future capabilities in this area in light of the limitations imposed by Resolutions 687, 707, and 715.

---

[1] Resolution 707, passed on August 15, 1991, requires Iraq, *inter alia*, to "provide full, final and complete disclosure" of "all aspects" of its nuclear, chemical, and biological weapons and ballistic missile programs and related facilities, to allow UN inspectors "unconditional and unrestricted access" to all "areas, facilities, equipment, records and means of transportation which they may wish to inspect." Iraq must cease immediately "any attempt to conceal, or any movement or destruction of any material or equipment" relating to these programs, and to "halt all nuclear activities of any kind," except the "use of isotopes for medical, agricultural or industrial purpose." UN, S/RES/707 (1991), August 15, 1991.

[2] Resolution 715, passed on October 11, 1991, requires Iraq to "meet unconditionally all its obligations" as outlined in the plans for "ongoing monitoring and verification" of Iraq's compliance with Resolutions 687 and 707. UN, S/RES/715 (1991), October 11, 1991. The plan for ongoing monitoring and verification can be found in UN documents S/22871/Rev. 1 and S/22872/Rev.1 and Corr.1.

NUCLEAR WEAPONS

Iraq's nuclear weapons program was the linchpin of its drive to become a regional power. It spared no effort in this area, employing some 20,000 people (including 7,000 scientists) and spending up to $12 billion on its crash program to acquire nuclear weapons. Iraq was pursuing three parallel routes to the bomb—calutron (EMIS), gas centrifuge, and chemical enrichment—and it had investigated several other paths, including plutonium separation, gaseous diffusion, laser, and jet nozzle enrichment. Its plans called for the eventual production of up to twenty nuclear weapons a year. On the eve of the Gulf War, it was two to three years from producing its first device.[1]

Thanks to coalition air strikes during the Gulf War and the subsequent efforts of UN weapons inspectors, Iraq's acknowledged nuclear program has been dismantled. However, gaps in our knowledge about the program make it impossible to assess its current status with certainty.[2] Iraqi statements and actions, however, leave no doubt that Saddam remains committed to acquiring a nuclear capability.[3] Iraq has tried to preserve surviving components of its nuclear weapons program; it possesses a cadre of skilled and experienced personnel with the know-how to make nuclear weapons as well as dual-use equipment which could be used to build them, and there are indications that it may be trying to acquire

---

[1] David Kay, "Iraqi Inspections: Lessons Learned," *Eye on Supply*, Winter 1993, pp. 88, 93, 98; Jay Davis and David Kay, "Iraq's Secret Nuclear Weapons Program," *Physics Today*, July 1992, p. 21; Paul Lewis, "U.N. Experts Now Say Baghdad Was Far From Making an A-Bomb Before Gulf War," *NYT*, May 20, 1992, p. A6.

[2] Peter D. Zimmerman, "Iraq's Nuclear Achievements: Components, Sources, and Stature," Congressional Research Service Report, June 4, 1993, pp. 12, 35-37.

[3] See for instance: Gary Milhollin, "Building Saddam's Bomb," *The New York Times Magazine*, March 8, 1992, pp. 30-36; Gary Milhollin, "The Iraqi Bomb," *The New Yorker*, February 1, 1993, pp. 47-56; David Kay, "Bomb Shelter: A Report from Iraq," *The New Republic*, March 15, 1993, pp. 11-13.

materials to support an ongoing clandestine research and development effort.[1]

Early Efforts

Iraq's nuclear program was initially based at the Tuwaitha Nuclear Research Center (which is about 20km southeast of Baghdad) and dates to the acquisition of the Soviet 14 Tammuz (IRT-5000) 5MW research reactor. This reactor became operational in 1968 and was originally engaged in medical and other civilian research. The program gained momentum in 1974 when Iraq signed a nuclear cooperation accord with France, which was followed by a 1976 contract for the 17 Tammuz nuclear research facility which consisted of two nuclear reactors: the Tammuz I (Osiraq) 70MW research reactor and the smaller Tammuz II 800KW research reactor. These deals were followed by the purchase of the 30 Tammuz research facility from Italy in 1978, which included a fuel reprocessing laboratory in which plutonium could be separated from spent uranium reactor fuel or irradiated natural uranium.[2] Although Iraq's intentions at Tuwaitha remain unclear, the infrastructure it established there in the late 1970s would have enabled it to pursue the plutonium route to the bomb had it been willing to violate its commitments as a signatory to the Nuclear Non-Proliferation Treaty. The Osiraq reactor was destroyed during the Israeli air strike in June 1981 and never rebuilt, while the Tammuz II and IRT-5000 reactors were destroyed by coalition air strikes during the Gulf War in January 1991.

---

[1] For instance, recent Iraqi attempts to purchase hydrofluoric acid—a chemical used in the production of the uranium hexafluoride feedstock used in the gas centrifuge and other enrichment processes and as a purging agent to remove industrial residues from centrifuge and calutron parts—raises questions about the current status of Iraq's nuclear program. *WP*, August 10, 1993, p. A6.

[2] Jed C. Snyder, "The Road to Osiraq: Baghdad's Quest for the Bomb," *The Middle East Journal*, Autumn 1983, pp. 565-593.

After Osiraq

Following the Osiraq raid, Iraq investigated a range of alternate routes to the bomb, finally focusing on calutron, gas centrifuge, and chemical enrichment as the most promising paths. In addition, Iraq now set as its goal the achievement of total self-sufficiency in all aspects of the production of nuclear weapons, including the development of indigenous sources of uranium, the production of fissile materials, and weapon design and development. In addition, it took elaborate steps to disperse and conceal its program to reduce the likelihood of detection and its vulnerability to bombing.

Iraq's calutron program dates to 1982. It was the most advanced of the three enrichment programs and was expected to yield three to four weapons a year.[1] Because the calutron program was an almost completely indigenous effort, details about it did not come to light until after the war with the defection of an Iraqi nuclear scientist to coalition forces in northern Iraq.[2] The calutron program had reached an advanced stage before work was interrupted by the war. Initial installation of separator units at Tarmiya commenced in January 1990 and by the time the Gulf War began, eight were operating and had yielded minute quantities of low enriched uranium. Plans called for a total of seventy first-stage and twenty second-stage separators to be installed at Tarmiya. A sister facility at Sharqat was expected to be completed thereafter. Performing at full capacity and reasonable efficiency, the calutron program could have produced about 30kg of highly enriched uranium per year—enough for one to two bombs. This would have provided Iraq with a near-term, albeit rather limited, initial production capability.[3]

---

[1] Kay, *op cit.,* p. 98.

[2] *WT,* June 11, 1991, pp. A1, A4; *NYT,* June 15, 1991, pp. A1, A5.

[3] Anthony Fainberg, "Strengthening IAEA Safeguards: Lessons from Iraq," Center for International Security and Arms Control, Stanford University, April 1993, p. 14. By contrast, Davis and Kay, *op cit.,* p. 25, put the production capacity of Tarmiya *alone* at 15-30kg per year—enough for one or two bombs. For more on the calutron program, see: UNSC, "Report on the Fourth IAEA On-Site Inspections in Iraq," (hereafter

Iraq's gas centrifuge program also dates to 1982; however, large-scale development work did not start until 1987, apparently following a decision to accelerate and expand the scope of the nuclear program.[1] The heart of the centrifuge program consisted of the al-Furat centrifuge production facility which was nearly completed when the Gulf War began (it was not bombed during the war). Moreover, although Iraq was still several years from completing its first centrifuge enrichment facility, it may have had an operational pilot cascade of 100-200 units.[2]

Iraq was working on two principal centrifuge prototypes based on the West European URENCO design (probably derived from purloined plans) and it apparently benefited from foreign assistance in their design and development.[3] Iraq had acquired from Germany and Switzerland sufficient quantities of custom-made components (centrifuge endcaps, cylinders, and rotors) and special materials (such as maraging steel) for an enrichment facility with up to 10,000 units (the planned production capacity of al-Furat is estimated at 2,000 units per year). The exact size and location of the planned centrifuge enrichment facility and the timetable for its operation remain unknown. However, a 10,000 unit facility operating at design levels could have produced more than 125kg of highly enriched uranium per year—enough for five to ten bombs.[4] The centrifuge program thus promised in the long-run to provide Iraq with a significant nuclear weapons production capability.

Finally, Iraq conducted research on chemical enrichment. This effort concentrated on the French CHEMEX solvent extraction method, although little is known about this program

---

IAEA-4), S/22986, August 28, 1991, pp. 5-9; IAEA-7, S/23215, November 14, 1991, pp. 22, 45-48.

[1] Kay, *op cit.*, p. 98; IAEA-15, S/24981, December 17, 1992, p. 11.

[2] Zimmerman, *op cit.*, p. 11.

[3] *ST*, December 16, 1990, pp. 4-5.

[4] Calculations based on estimates in Kay, *op cit.*, 88, 98. See also: IAEA-4, S/22986, July 27-August 10, 1991, pp. 9-13; IAEA-7, S/23215, November 14, 1991, pp. 8, 19-23, 49-52.

since the Iraqis razed the Tuwaitha laboratory engaged in this research before inspectors were able to visit it.[1]

Although the calutron and gas centrifuge programs were pursued independently, it is likely that once the gas centrifuge enrichment program came on line—with its greater potential annual production capacity—the calutrons would then have been used as a topping cycle to do final enrichment of feedstock partially enriched by gas centrifuges. This would have permitted greater total yields of highly-enriched uranium than would have been possible had the two programs operated independently.[2]

On the eve of the war, weapon design work had also progressed to a relatively advanced stage. Iraq had completed at least five different designs for an implosion device with a 20kt yield (the size of the Hiroshima bomb) which was to be mounted on a missile, and had also made significant strides toward reducing the size and weight of the weapon. Work had begun on a detonation and firing system and on initiators. There are also indications that the Iraqis were interested in eventually producing thermonuclear and boosted-yield weapons. Weaponization work was done at al-Athir—the center of the design and development effort—and al-Tuwaitha, with testing of the explosives package done at the Hittin, al-Qa'qa', and al-Hatra explosives test ranges.[3]

Unanswered Questions

Although Iraq's acknowledged nuclear program has been dismantled, it is impossible to be certain that undeclared facilities do not remain. Speculation has focused on the possible existence of an underground reactor and centrifuge cascade.

There are a number of reasons to believe that Iraq may have been building an unsafeguarded underground nuclear reactor

---

[1] Davis and Kay, *op cit.*, p. 22.

[2] Davis and Kay, *op cit.*, p. 22.

[3] Kay, *op cit.*, pp. 88-89; Zimmerman, *op cit.*, pp. 20-23; and UNSC, *Report of the Executive Chairman*, S/23165, October 25, 1991, p. 23.

for the production of plutonium:[1] 1) plutonium offers the easiest and quickest route to the bomb, as well as a number of advantages (such as reduced size and weight), making it ideal for missile delivery; 2) before terminatinating negotiations, Iraq had, in fact, aquired design data from the Soviet Union, the PRC, and France in the early 1980s for an underground reactor and could have used this data to design its own reactor; 3) UN inspectors discovered two separate cases of plutonium reprocessing involving the IRT-5000 reactor, indicating continued interest in the plutonium route as late as 1990.[2]

Concerns that Iraq may have a hidden pilot gas centrifuge cascade derive from the fact that Iraq had purchased components for about 10,000 gas centrifuges; some believe that it would not have done so unless it had a proven centrifuge design which had been validated through testing in a pilot cascade.[3]

None of the efforts by UN inspectors to locate an underground reactor or a centrifuge cascade have, to date, met with success.

Toward the Future—Ongoing Concerns

Iraq will face formidable obstacles to reviving its nuclear program. Its nuclear infrastructure has been largely, if not completely, dismantled, sanctions significantly complicate the

---

[1] Informed opinion differs on this issue. Former IAEA inspector David Kay has made a strong case for the existence of an underground reactor. See Kay, *op cit.*, pp. 97-98. On the other hand, current IAEA inspector Bob Kelley has stated that "[after having] analyzed a huge body of data on this subject...there is no reason to believe there is a hidden reactor in Iraq." Leon Barkho, "U.N. Closes File of Hidden Reactor in Iraq," *Reuters*, June 30, 1993.

[2] For additional details see: Kay, *op cit.*, pp. 97-98.

[3] However, because Iraq tended to purchase equipment for its nonconventional weapons programs in bulk quantities as opportunities presented themselves (since the export of many of these components were illegal), it is possible that the Iraqis purchased centrifuge components even before they had a validated centrifuge design. Jon B. Wolfsthal and Matthew Bunn, "Ambassador Rolf Ekeus: Unearthing Iraq's Arsenal," *ACT*, April 1992, p. 9.

acquisition of sensitive technology abroad, and the intrusive presence of UN weapons inspectors will constrain future efforts. On the other hand, Iraq retains the most important assets required to rebuild its nuclear program: a cadre of skilled and experienced managers, scientists, and technicians; possibly sizable inventories of undeclared equipment, machine tools[1], and special materials; and, a viable nuclear weapon design.

Iraq can be expected to take even more elaborate steps than it did in the past to ensure the secrecy and survivability of the program. In order to prevent a repetition of Israel's destruction of its Osiraq reactor in 1981, Iraq redesigned its nuclear program—dispersing and concealing its nuclear facilities. Iraq initially considered the possibility of building an underground reactor in order to protect it from air strikes and satellite detection, and Belgian, Chinese, Finnish, French, Italian, and Soviet companies were requested to make an assessment of this possibility.[2]

Moreover, Iraq's calutron enrichment facility at Tarmiya incorporated an elaborate and costly air filtration system to reduce or eliminate particulate emissions which could have signaled nuclear activity at the site. Power lines to Tarmiya were buried to eliminate indicators of the energy intensive calutron program, while there were no air defenses or security fences around the site (because it was located in a large military exclusion zone) which might have drawn the attention of photo-interpreters.[3] At a sister site at Sharqat, buildings were deliberately built to a different configuration to

---

[1] Iraq may still possess thousands of dual-use machine tools because the exact number it purchased is unknown (many sales—since they were illegal—were never properly registered). Of 2,000 machine tools *known* to have been exported to Iraq by the UK, Germany, Italy, and others, only 600 have been found. Kenneth R. Timmerman, "Iraq Rebuilds its Military Industries," House Foreign Affairs Committee, June 29, 1993, pp. 8-9.

[2] IAEA-10, S/23644, February 26, 1992, pp. 3-4; IAEA-20/21, S/26333, August 20, 1993, p. 14; The Nuclear Control Institute, Press Release: "Declassified U.S. Intelligence Report Reveals Chinese Nuclear Assistance to Iraq," July 1, 1991.

[3] Kay, *op cit.*, p. 91.

reduce the likelihood that the two sites would be linked in the event that one of the sites was compromised.

Finally, except for the most senior managers, contact between personnel involved in different components of the program was stringently regulated and information concerning the various parts of the program was strictly compartmentalized. Iraqi scientists, when they traveled abroad, did so under assumed names and were accompanied by security personnel—as much to protect them as to keep an eye on them.[1]

The Iraqi experience during the Gulf War and with UN weapons inspectors afterward is likely to galvanize Iraq's future nuclear efforts in much the way the Osiraq bombing did more than a decade ago. A revived program is likely to be even more difficult to detect or disrupt, since it will be designed from the ground up to escape detection and survive air or missile strikes. The Iraqis will bring to this effort a detailed understanding of methods to conceal their activities from foreign intelligence agencies, exploit the limitations of the UN's ongoing monitoring and verification efforts, and minimize the effects of bombing on facilities and equipment.[2] Specific steps Iraq is likely to take in the future could include:

• Greater efforts at dispersing, camouflaging, and concealing facilities, and locating and constructing buildings to minimize vulnerability to air attacks—including increased reliance on underground facilities and the use of blast walls.[3]

---

[1] WP, October 13, 1991, p. A44.

[2] See for instance, Kay, op cit., p. 91; WP, November 3, 1991, p. C1.

[3] The dispersal of industrial facilities, the construction of underground plants, and the use of blast walls were standard measures taken by Germany during World War II to increase the survivability of its industries in response to allied bombing. See: USSBS, Overall Report (European War), September 30, 1945, pp. 29, 41-45 87-89; USSBS Aircraft Division Industry Report, November 2, 1945, pp. 7-10, 86-87, 90-93, 98-99, 109-110, 114, 117-119. Iraq is known to have a number of underground industrial facilities. One of these—an underground oil refinery located near Sharqat—was discovered by IAEA weapons inspectors looking for an

• Increased emphasis on emission control and signature reduction, particularly of heat discharges, penetrating radiation, isotopic effluents, electronic communications, and vehicular and pedestrian traffic which could betray proscribed activities.[1]

• The construction of facilities configured to permit the rapid removal of critical equipment and machinery and their dispersal to secure areas in the event of air or missile attack, building on past successes in this area.[2]

• Decreased reliance on large, high-profile, permanent facilities which are easy to detect and destroy, and increased reliance where possible on small and inconspicuous temporary or makeshift facilities for weapons design, development, and testing.[3]

---

underground nuclear reactor. IAEA-14, S/24593, September 28, 1992, pp. 4, 9.

[1] For instance, heat signatures could be reduced by building smaller facilities and investing in heat sinking and cooling systems; penetrating radiation could be reduced by shielding; and isotopic effluents could be reduced by using more efficient air and water filters. Fainberg, *op cit.*, pp. 20-41.

[2] According to one visitor to Iraq, specialized equipment such as computers and electronics had been removed from obvious civilian and military targets before the Gulf War. As a result, in many cases only buildings were destroyed. Following the war, many of these facilities were rapidly rebuilt, equipment was reinstalled, and the facilities were quickly put back into service. *AW&ST*, January 27, 1992, p. 62. Likewise, prior to the U.S. cruise missile strike on the General Intelligence headquarters in Baghdad in late June 1993, many strategic industrial facilities and government buildings were stripped of critical equipment, machinery, records, and files, and personnel were told to stay home indefinitely in anticipation of the attack. *NYT*, July 15, 1993, p. A3.

[3] According to one UN official, Iraqi nuclear scientists have already indicated that in the future they will eschew large, vulnerable facilities in favor of small, dispersed, and more survivable facilities. In addition, some inspectors believe that many of Iraq's nuclear research facilities were more sophisticated than needed to design an early generation bomb. Iraq could have instead made do with moveable trailers and a bulldozer to create temporary sites for testing the bomb's explosives package. When done, they could have then leveled the site and moved

While these steps will inevitably raise the costs and slow the progress of a nuclear weapons program, they are likely to be seen as necessary trade-offs required to ensure the secrecy and survivability of the program.

The task of monitoring and verifying Iraqi compliance with UN resolutions would become even more difficult should Saddam bar UN inspectors from Iraq or take steps to further reduce their freedom of movement. Direct detection techniques, such as on-site inspections and environmental sampling—part of the ongoing monitoring effort[1]—are almost without exception more sensitive and reliable than remote detection means such as aerial or satellite reconnaissance.[2]

Moreover, the collapse of the Soviet Union may provide Iraq with an unprecedented opportunity to acquire nuclear weapons or devices, fissile material, and technical expertise, thus allowing Iraq to revive its nuclear program. For instance:

- A breakdown in the system of control over nuclear weapons in the former Soviet Union might enable Iraq to acquire tactical nuclear weapons (such as bombs or artillery rounds) in order to create a small nuclear arsenal, or they

---

the trailers to a motor pool, leaving few if any traces of their activities. Zimmerman, *op cit.,* p. 28.

[1] Direct detection techniques used in Iraq include visual observation and the collection of samples of industrial materials and residues, water, and sediment for laboratory analysis. For details, see: D.L. Donohue and R. Zeisler, "Behind the Scenes: Scientific Analysis of Samples from Nuclear Inspections in Iraq," IAEA Bulletin, 1/1992, pp. 25-32; Breck W. Henderson, "Livermore Combats Spread of Nuclear Arms," *AW&ST*, November 2, 1992, pp. 60-61. As part of the ongoing monitoring effort, UN inspectors conducted a comprehensive radiometric survey of the surface waters of Iraq during IAEA-14 and -15 (in September and December 1992) to establish a baseline against which future sampling results will be compared. Inspectors believe that this is an almost foolproof method for detecting major prohibited nuclear activities. IAEA-14, S/24593, September 28, 1992, pp. 9-11; IAEA-15, S/24981, December 17, 1992, pp. 6-7, 9.

[2] David Fulghum, "Advanced Arms Spread Defies Remote Detection," *AW&ST*, November 9, 1992, pp. 20-21; and Fainberg, *op cit.,* pp. 21-41.

could be dismantled and exploited as a source of fissile material and components.[1]

• The emergence of a black market for nuclear materials from the former Soviet bloc raises the possibility of the unauthorized transfer of fissile material (weapons grade uranium or plutonium). While there is as of yet no evidence that significant quantities of fissile material have been smuggled, the potential for undetected transfers warrants concern.[2]

• There have been unconfirmed reports that Iraq has hired some fifty Russian nuclear scientists to work on their nuclear program.[3] These scientists could help their Iraqi colleagues evaluate past efforts and resolve technical bottlenecks in their program.

The acquisition of fissile material abroad would solve the main obstacle to the production of a nuclear weapon by Iraq. It already has experienced personnel, undeclared inventories of equipment, machine tools, special materials, and a viable bomb design; the possibility that it could build a weaponization infrastructure with resources still on hand thus cannot be completely dismissed. In addition, if weapons development and testing were to be restricted to small and inconspicuous facilities, such an effort might escape detection by UN inspectors. Facilities handling weapons grade uranium and plutonium can be shielded to prevent telltale penetrating radiation that could compromise such an effort.[4]

Finally, because UN Resolution 707 permits the use of isotopes for medicine, agriculture, and industry, Iraq could

---

[1] Richard Garwin, "Post-Soviet Nuclear Command and Security," *ACT*, January/February 1992, pp. 19-21.

[2] William C. Potter, "Nuclear Exports From the Former Soviet Union: What's New, What's True," *ACT*, January/February 1993, pp. 3-10.

[3] *Morgenpost Am Sonntag*, March 1, 1992, p. 2, in *JPRS-TND*, March 13, 1992, p. 20; and *Izvestiya*, October 20, 1992, p. 7, in *FBIS-SOV*, October 22, 1992, p. 4.

[4] David Hughes, "Arms Experts Fear Nuclear Blackmail," *AW&ST*, January 4, 1993, p. 61.

produce radiological weapons that could threaten enemy population centers. (A radiological weapon may be nothing more than a bomb or missile warhead filled with hazardous radioactive materials.)[1] While there is no evidence that Iraq has pursued this option in the past, it remains a threat that cannot be dismissed.[2]

CHEMICAL AND BIOLOGICAL WEAPONS

Before the Gulf War, Iraq had the most advanced and diverse chemical warfare program in the Arab world. It commenced large-scale production of chemical weapons in 1984 and by the time of the Gulf War, Iraq could produce 1,000 tons of chemical agents annually (although actual production was significantly less),[3] including the nerve agents sarin (GB and a GB/GF admixture) and the blister agent mustard (HD).[4]

---

[1] Compounding these concerns, IAEA inspector Maurizio Zifferero has stated that "there is no reason why Iraq should not be allowed to pursue legitimate civilian nuclear research again. I can imagine the day where they might want to rebuild the Tuwaitha research reactor, or build nuclear power plants." *MEDNEWS*, January 25, 1993, p. 2. These steps would even further increase the risk of Iraq developing radiological weapons.

[2] According to a recently released Russian Foreign Intelligence Service report, during the Gulf War a high level Soviet "crisis [working] group" concluded that the "possibility of Iraq's use of radiological weapons...could not be ruled out." The study goes on to say that the disaster at Chernobyl may have increased the incentives for developing and using radiological weapons for certain states, and that the proliferation of radiological weapons may be an unavoidable consequence of the worldwide spread of nuclear materials and technology. Foreign Intelligence Service, *Proliferation of Weapons of Mass Destruction*, p. 23.

[3] To date, about 500 tons of agent (355 tons in bulk storage and the remainder in munitions) and 3,500 tons of precursors have been recovered or accounted for.

[4] Michael Eisenstadt, *"Sword of the Arabs:" Iraq's Strategic Weapons*, Policy Paper No. 21 (Washington, D.C.: The Washington Institute for Near East Policy, August 1990), pp. 5-9. The Iraqis refer to the GB/GF admixture as binary sarin. Iraq also produced limited quantities of tabun (GA) although it reportedly ceased production in 1986, and was investigating the production of the persistent nerve agents soman (GD) and VX. UN Press Release, IK/27, June 24, 1991, p. 2.

Iraq's principal chemical agent production facility was located at Samarra; it included research and development, production, munitions manufacturing, filling, and storing facilities. Munitions produced included missile warheads, bombs, and tube and rocket artillery.[1] Chemical agents were produced from precursors procured abroad (from firms in Austria, Belgium, Germany, Holland, India, Italy, Spain, Switzerland, and the United States), as well as small quantities manufactured at Falluja, where three production lines were built to produce nerve agent precursors.[2] Chemical weapons were stockpiled at Samarra and at air bases and ammunition storage depots around the country.[3] The Samarra complex was heavily damaged during the war.

The picture is less clear with regard to Iraq's biological weapons program. Some reports claim that Iraq had successfully weaponized anthrax and botulin toxin and in 1989 initiated large-scale production of missile warheads, bombs, and rocket artillery filled with these agents.[4] Other reports point to the fact that neither weapons nor agents have been recovered to support the claim that Iraq had not yet reached this point by the time of the Gulf War.[5]

---

[1] Chemical weapons produced by Iraq include al-Husayn missile warheads (unitary and binary sarin), five types of bombs (unitary and binary sarin, mustard, and CS), 155mm artillery rounds (mustard), 122mm rocket artillery rounds (unitary sarin), and 120mm mortar rounds (CS). Terry Gander, "Iraq: The Chemical Arsenal," *JIR*, September 1992, pp. 414-415.

[2] While one of the precursor production lines at Falluja was never completed, a second produced limited quantities of chlorine compounds starting in 1990, while a third was dedicated to the production of pesticides. All three production lines were heavily damaged during the Gulf War. UNSC, *Report by the Executive Chairman*, S/23165, October 25, 1991, p. 27.

[3] Eliot A. Cohen and Thomas A. Keaney, *Gulf War Air Power Survey: Summary Report* (Washington, D.C.: Government Printing Office, 1993), pp. 80-81.

[4] DoD, *Conduct of the Persian Gulf War*, April 1992, p. 15.

[5] Maj. Karen Jansen, "Biological Weapons Proliferation," in Steven Mataija and J. Marshall Beier (Eds.), *Multilateral Verification and the Post-Gulf Environment: Learning from the UNSCOM Experience* (York University:

Iraq acknowledges that it commenced research into biological warfare agents in 1986. It also admits that it worked on two biological warfare agents—anthrax and botulin toxin— and that it conducted military research that could serve both defensive and offensive purposes with three micro-organisms—bacillus anthraxus, clostridium botulinum, and clostridium perfringens—although it claims that all stocks have been destroyed (a claim which is impossible to verify).[1]

Iraq's primary biological warfare research complex at Salman Pak—which was heavily damaged during the war— had the capability to research, produce, test, and store biological warfare agents. Fermentation facilities capable of producing fifty gallons of anthrax bacteria a week, as well as production, aerosol testing, and storage facilities existed at the site. However, neither agents, munitions, nor munitions filling facilities were found there.[2] A second facility which almost certainly was intended as Iraq's primary biological warfare production facility—al-Hakam—was located near Musayib (it had not been completed by the time the Gulf War began).[3] In addition, more than twenty specially designed refrigerated bunkers for the storage of biological or other special weapons were scattered around the country.[4]

Centre for International and Strategic Studies, December 1992), pp. 111, 114.

[1] Iraq also provided UN inspectors with bacterial seed stocks for four biological warfare agents—brucellus abortus, brucella melitensis, francisella tularensis, and clostridium botulinum, and for the biological warfare agent simulents bacillus subtilis, bacillis cereus, and bacillus megaterium. UNSC, *Report of the Executive Chairman,* S/23165, October 25, 1991, p. 30.

[2] UN Press Release, IK/46, August 14, 1991, p. 1.

[3] The al-Hakam probable biological warfare production facility near Musayib now serves as an animal feed plant and is being monitored by UN inspectors to ensure that it is not used for the production of biological warfare agents in the future. Jansen, *op cit.,* pp. 113-114; UN Press Release, IK/69, October 31, 1991, p. 2.

[4] DoD, *op cit.,* p. 15; *GWAPS, op cit.,* p. 82. Facilities suspected of being involved in the biological warfare program before the war (such as the so-called baby milk factory at Abu Ghurayb as well as other facilities at Latifiya and Taji), were bombed during the war. It now appears that none of these were in fact connected with the biological warfare

Iraq has taken great efforts to preserve surviving components of its biological warfare program. It retains the know-how to produce biological weapons and is believed to have saved critical production equipment as well as seed stocks for producing agents. Consequently, despite sanctions and UN inspections, Iraq could probably produce biological agents at this time. Such an effort would have a low likelihood of detection since a clandestine biological warfare production facility would be small and inconspicuous, and provide few if any distinct signatures to be detected by foreign intelligence agencies.[1]

Iraq's surviving biological warfare capability is a source of particular concern. Biological weapons can inflict truly massive casualties, and are much more lethal than chemical weapons, providing the broadest area coverage per pound of any weapon system. In this respect, biological weapons have the potential to be true weapons of mass destruction.[2]

---

program. Office of History, 37th Fighter Wing, "Nighthawks Over Iraq: A Chronology of the F-117A Stealth Fighter in Operations Desert Shield and Desert Storm," Special Study: 37FW/HO-91-1, 1991.

[1] Jonathan B. Tucker, "The Future of Biological Warfare," in W. Thomas Wander and Eric H. Arnett, *The Proliferation of Advanced Weaponry: Technology, Motivations, and Responses* (Washington, D.C.: American Association for the Advancement of Science, 1992), p. 61. In recent public testimony, CIA director James Woolsey claimed that of all of Iraq's unconventional weapons programs, its "biological weapons capability is perhaps of greatest immediate concern" since "neither war nor inspections have seriously degraded this capability." Woolsey, *op cit.*, p. 9.

[2] According to a DoD assessment, experimental data indicates that a SCUD-B missile warhead filled with botulin toxin "could contaminate an area of 3,700 square kilometers (based on ideal weather conditions and an effective dispersal mechanism), or sixteen times greater than the same warhead filled with sarin." By the time symptoms appear, "treatment has little chance of success" since "rapid field detection methods for biological warfare agents do not exist." DoD, *Conduct of the War*, p. 15. According to a World Health Organization assessment, "an attack on a city" involving 50kg of dried anthrax "in a suitable aerosol form" could affect an area "far in excess of twenty square kilometers" and cause "tens to hundreds of thousands of deaths." WHO, *Health Aspects of Chemical and Biological Weapons* (Geneva: WHO, 1970), p. 19.

It is not clear, however, whether Iraq has successfully weaponized biological warfare agents and overcome the technical obstacles to their effective delivery and dispersal. As a result, Iraq might prefer to use terrorist surrogates to deliver biological warfare agents it might possess against enemy civilian population centers via public water supplies or the ventilation systems of major buildings or subway systems. This means that delivery is simple and effective, and does not entail many of the technical difficulties which make the battlefield employment of biological warfare agents so problematic.[1] Iraq's continued involvement in international terrorism and its residual biological warfare capability are thus a potentially dangerous combination that will remain a source of concern in the future.

Although Iraq's known chemical weapon production capability has been dismantled, it retains the know-how to produce chemical weapons and may have saved some critical production equipment. It would almost certainly revive its chemical warfare program if given the opportunity, since chemical weapons offer a proven capability that was used to great effect during the Iran-Iraq War.

Iraq may also have stocks of biological and chemical weapons and agents produced before the Gulf War. Anthrax spores can last for decades under certain conditions. By contrast, most biological agents can be stored in a refrigerated facility for three to six months; after that time they lose their virulence and viability, necessitating new production to replace old stocks.[2] Thus, Iraq may have stocks of anthrax from its pre-war program. And while most of Iraq's stocks of sarin and mustard agent were of poor quality and deteriorated in storage, some high quality stocks of mustard agent that remained viable were recovered.[3] Thus, Iraq may have stocks

---

[1] For details about the problems of weaponization and dispersal, see: W. Seth Carus, *"The Poor Man's Atomic Bomb?" Biological Weapons in the Middle East*, Policy Paper No. 23 (Washington, D.C.: The Washington Institute for Near East Policy, 1991), pp. 31-41.

[2] Tucker, *op cit.*, pp. 67-68.

[3] UN Press Release, IK/72, November 20, 1991, pp. 1-2.

of anthrax and mustard agents produced before the Gulf War which it is saving for future contingencies.

BALLISTIC MISSILES AND SUPERGUNS

Before the Gulf War, Iraq was developing a range of missiles and superguns to deliver conventional and nonconventional payloads against enemy population centers throughout the region.

Iraq's strategic missile program consisted of four main elements: 1) the Badr 2000 missile; 2) the al-Husayn missile and its derivatives; 3) the Faw cruise missile; and 4) efforts to modify various Soviet surface-to-air missile for use against ground targets.[1]

The Badr 2000 was a 1,000km range two-staged solid-fuel missile capable of carrying a 500kg warhead. It was intended to serve as Iraq's primary nuclear delivery system, although FAE warheads were also reportedly considered.[2] The Badr 2000 was initially developed in conjunction with Argentina, where it was known as the Condor II, and Egypt where it was called the Vector.[3] As a result of U.S. pressure, Egypt pulled out of the joint program in 1988 and Argentina withdrew in 1989. Iraq continued with its own program until work was halted by the Gulf War, before a prototype missile could be produced. Facilities for the production of the Badr 2000 first stage and motor were located at the Dhu al-Fiqar factory at Falluja (motor cases and nozzles), the Taj al-Ma'arik factory at Latifiya (solid fuel mixing and casting), and the al-Yawm al-'Azim factory at

---

[1] Iraq also produced a prototype satellite launch vehicle—the al-'Abid—which consisted of a booster stage of five clustered SCUD-B rocket motors, a second stage consisting of a SCUD-B rocket motor, and a third stage consisting of a modified SA-2 missile. Its maiden and sole test flight in December 1989 was unsuccessful. William Lowther, *Arms and the Man: Dr. Gerald Bull, Iraq, and the Supergun* (New York: Ivy Books, 1991), pp. 174-176, 200, 207, 250-251.

[2] Simon Henderson, *Instant Empire: Saddam Hussein's Ambitions for Iraq* (San Francisco: Mercury House, 1991), pp. 128-130; Alan George, "A Bigger Blast," *The Middle East*, January 1991, pp. 15-16.

[3] Joseph S. Bermudez Jr., "Ballistic Missile Development in Egypt," *JIR*, October 1992, pp. 456-458.

Musayib (motor assembly and testing). Facilities to produce the Badr 2000 second stage and warhead had not yet been built when the Gulf War broke out.

The mainstay of Iraq's strategic missile force was the al-Husayn, which was based on the SCUD-B; it had a range of 650km and mounted both conventional and chemical warheads.[1] It was produced in large numbers—more than 400 in all—and was used extensively toward the end of the Iran-Iraq War and during the Gulf War.[2] Iraq may still have undeclared inventories of these missiles as well as mobile launchers.[3]

However, Iraq probably does not have the liquid fuel and oxidizer needed to launch these missiles. Its entire stock was procured from the former Soviet Union, and because both fuel and oxidizer have a shelf life of about twelve to eighteen months, fresh batches must be procured periodically to replace

---

[1] Iraq admits to having produced ninety-five chemical warheads for its al-Husayn missiles, including both unitary and binary-type sarin variants. UN Press Release, IK/98, April 3, 1992, p. 1. Because these warheads were contact fused (which would have resulted in ground bursts and poor dissemination of the chemical agent), and were poorly constructed, there are doubts about how effective they would have been if used. Gander, *op cit.*, p. 415.

[2] About 189 were launched during the Iran-Iraq War and eighty-eight during the Gulf War. W. Seth Carus and Joseph S. Bermudez Jr., "Iraq's Al-Husayn Missile Programme," *JIR*, May 1990, pp. 204-209; *JIR*, June 1990, pp. 242-248; UN Press Release, IK/128, November 5, 1992, p. 1. Iraq also produced a small number of al-Hijara (750km) and al-'Abbas (900km) missiles; these were extended-range variants of the al-Husayn which never entered into series production. It had also developed a concept for a missile called the Tammuz I which was a 2,000km range two-stage missile consisting of a single extended range SCUD-B booster rocket topped by a modified SA-2 second stage.

[3] See Appendix I. Iraq has acknowledged having a total of nineteen mobile launchers (ten Soviet MAZ-543 TELs, six al-Nida' MELs, and three al-Walids MELs) and nine decoy launchers. Iraq had also built twenty-eight fixed launchers in the western part of the country and planned to build another twenty-eight there. Individual fixed launch sites were also located at Taji, Baghdad (Saddam Airfield), and Daura. UN Press Release, IK/79, December 18, 1991, p. 1; UN Press Release, IK/128, November 5, 1992, pp. 1-2.

or renew expired stocks. Thus, any undeclared stocks of fuel and oxidizer Iraq may possess are probably no longer viable, although it might be able to obtain small quantities of fresh fuel and oxidizer on the international black market.

Production facilities associated with the al-Husayn program were located at the Nasr missile factory at Taji (which was destroyed during the Gulf War) and included a warhead plant, a guidance system workshop, and an airframe plant. A mobile launcher workshop associated with the program was located at Daura.[1]

The Faw cruise missile was an extended-range HY-2 Silkworm anti-ship missile which may have been intended for use against ground targets. Three variants, with ranges of 75km, 150km, and 200km were under development at the Nasr missile factory at Taji, although work had not advanced beyond the design phase when the Gulf War broke out.[2]

Finally, Iraq had considered modifying a number of Soviet surface-to-air missiles for use against ground targets, including the SA-2 (Fahd 300 and 500), SA-3 (Baraq), and SA-6 (Kasir).[3]

---

[1] Project 144 was the Iraqi designation for the program based at the Nasr missile factory at Taji dedicated to extending the range of SCUD-B, HY-2 Silkworm, and SA-2 liquid-fuel missiles in its inventories. The al-Husayn and its variants were produced by cannibalizing or modifying SCUD-B missiles to expand the capacity of their fuel and oxidizer tanks, reducing the high-explosive payload carried in the warhead from about 1,000kg to 150-250kg, and modifying their guidance systems. Similar modifications were planned for the HY-2 (Faw) and SA-2 (Fahd) to extend the range of these missiles. Moreover, when the Gulf War broke out, efforts were under way to develop an indigenously produced version of the al-Husayn using locally produced and foreign—mainly German—components. *Der Spiegel,* January 28, 1991, pp. 3-4, in *JPRS-TND,* February 25, 1991, p. 49; *Der Spiegel,* November 18, 1991, pp. 41-52, in *FBIS-WEU,* November 21, 1991, pp. 11-14. Reverse engineering design studies of SCUD-B, HY-2, and SA-2 rocket motors for Project 144 were conducted at the Shahiyat liquid-fuel motor plant and test facility at al-Rafah; this effort was designated Project 1728 by the Iraqis.

[2] Christopher F. Foss (Ed.), *Jane's Armour and Artillery: 1989-90* (Coulsdon: Jane's Information Group, 1990), p. 728.

[3] *Al-Qabas,* June 16-17, 1990, p. 10.

Several SA-2s were tested in the surface-to-surface mode and a number of Fahd 300 prototypes were built. However, the effort was abandoned when it became clear that these modified missiles were too inaccurate to have much utility.

Since the war, Iraq has rebuilt its missile research and development infrastructure. The heart of this effort is located at the Ibn al-Haytham missile research and development center just north of Baghdad where work is being done on half a dozen different missiles with ranges less than 150km (which are permitted by Resolution 687), including the Ababil-50 and -100 artillery missiles, the Faw anti-ship cruise missile, and SA-2 and SA-3 surface-to-air missiles. A half-dozen facilities support this effort, including the al-Qa'qa' explosive plant (solid-fuel production), the Taj al-Ma'arik missile production facility (solid fuel mixing and casting), the al-Rafah missile test facility (liquid-fuel motor development and testing), and the al-Yawm al-'Azim missile production facility (solid-fuel motor testing). Although Iraq's current production capability is quite limited, UN inspectors believe that should inspections cease, Iraq could produce missiles with ranges greater than 150km by modifying or perhaps by clustering or stacking missiles currently under development.[1]

Iraq also continues to show interest in reviving its supergun program (Project Babylon)—underscoring its abiding desire to become a regional power. Before the Gulf War, Iraq was working on a family of superguns capable of firing rocket-assisted projectiles with unconventional payloads at targets more than 1,000km away.[2] Available evidence indicates that Iraq intended to build two guns with a 1,000mm bore and a 156 meter barrel, and two guns with a 350mm bore and a 46 meter barrel (a prototype of one of the smaller guns found at Jabal Hamrin was aimed at Israel and had been assembled and test

---

[1] See the interview with UNSCOM ballistic missile team leader Nikita Smidovich in *AFP*, June 4, 1993, in *FBIS-NES*, June 7, 1993, p. 31.
[2] Henderson, *op cit.*, pp. 142-154; Lowther, *op cit.*, pp. 181-184; *NYT*, July 1, 1993, p. A1.

fired).[1] Components for the superguns were produced in the United Kingdom, Belgium, Italy, Germany, Switzerland, Greece, and Spain.[2] However, the Martlet IV projectile being designed for the gun had never been completed and plans for it have never been found.[3] Recently there have been reports that Iraq has revived its efforts to build a 1,000mm supergun. According to these reports, Iraq has approached Russian firms to discuss the possibility of producing components for such a gun, and has tried to enlist the assistance of some of the foreign scientists and engineers involved in the original effort.[4]

CONCLUSIONS

Had the Gulf War not occurred, Iraq would have almost certainly been a nuclear power by now. It would also have a significant biological and chemical warfare capability and a range of delivery options, including missiles, strike aircraft, and superguns. Thanks to the Gulf War and and UN inspections, however, Iraq's acknowledged nuclear program has been dismantled (although there are indications that it may be planning to resurrect this program) and its biological and chemical warfare capabilities have been dramatically reduced. Iraq nonetheless remains a nonconventional threat and will continue to do so for the foreseeable future.

According to CIA estimates, if sanctions and UN inspections were to cease, Iraq would be able to produce nuclear weapons within five to seven years (much sooner if it were to acquire fissile material from abroad), restore its former chemical weapons production capability in less than one year, and produce militarily significant quantities of biological weapons in a matter of weeks (if it cannot already do so). Averting this scenario will be a major challenge for U.S. policy in the coming years.

---

[1] *WP,* July 20, 1991, p. A14; *JDW,* September 14, 1991, pp. 458-459. There are also reports that the Iraqis had considered a 600mm supergun as well. Henderson, *op cit.,* p. 153.

[2] Henderson, *op cit.,* pp. 150-151; Lowther, *op cit.,* p. 203.

[3] Lowther, *op cit.,* p. 270.

[4] *LST,* May 16, 1993.

Following the Gulf War, the UN moved to dismantle Iraq's nonconventional capabilities, along the lines of UN Resolutions 687 and 707, as well as Resolution 715, which approved the UN plan for ongoing monitoring and verification. Sanctions cannot be lifted until Iraq is found to be in compliance with 687 and 707 and the plan for ongoing monitoring and verification has been accepted by Iraq and is in place.

Resolutions 687 and 707 require Iraq to dismantle all its nonconventional weapons programs and provide complete details concerning all of its activities in this area. Resolution 715 requires Iraq to accept the plan for ongoing monitoring and verification of its compliance, through on-site inspections and aerial overflights by the UN, and the provision of information by Iraq. Resolution 687 links the lifting of the ban on oil sales to Iraq's compliance with those provisions requiring the dismantling of its nonconventional capabilities; it was believed that the linkage would serve as an incentive for Iraqi cooperation.

Iraq has not yet complied with Resolutions 687 and 707. It recently provided UNSCOM with new data during meetings in Baghdad in October 1993 concerning its missile and biological warfare programs and foreign suppliers, which UN officials claim brought it closer to compliance—although it may never be possible to verify Iraqi compliance with certainty. In addition, Iraq has thus far rejected Resolution 715, which it claims infringes on its independence and sovereignty.

Experience since the war, however, has raised serious doubts about whether the UN sanctions and monitoring regime can ultimately accomplish its intended objective—the dismantling of Iraq's nonconventional capabilities.

First, Resolution 687 is self-subverting; by linking the lifting of the ban on oil sales to the dismantling of Iraq's nonconventional weapons programs, the resolution contains the seeds of its own undoing. If the ban on oil sales is lifted (once UNSCOM has verified that Iraq is in compliance with Resolutions 687 and 707 and has accepted its obligations under the plan for ongoing monitoring and verification), Saddam Hussein's Iraq will earn billions of dollars and once again have the financial means to enlist corrupt foreign government officials and greedy businessmen in its efforts to smuggle whatever is required to rebuild its nonconventional capabilities; there is no way to be certain that these efforts will be detected. And, should the general ban on trade with Iraq be lifted, it will be even harder to regulate the flow of dual-use items into the country (or prevent their use for prohibited activities). The UN plan for ongoing monitoring and verification calls for the creation of a mechanism by which Iraq and its business partners will report the sale or supply of dual-use items in advance. The Iraqis, however, could easily subvert these safeguards by bribing unscrupulous businessmen not to report these transactions. In this way, Iraq might be able to rebuild its stock of dual-use equipment through overt (and clandestine) procurement under the cover provided by UN resolutions intended to prevent this very eventuality.

Second, because Resolution 707 permits Iraq to use isotopes for medical, agricultural, and industrial purposes, it offers Baghdad an opportunity to produce radiological weapons that could threaten civilian population centers throughout the region.

Third, the UN is not likely to detect Iraqi violations of Resolutions 687 and 707. Iraq will take stringent measures to hide its efforts to rebuild its nonconventional weapons programs and will bring to this effort detailed knowledge of the capabilities and limitations of the monitoring and verification means and methods available to the UN. Moreover, intelligence concerning Iraq's nonconventional programs has been uneven; because of the nature of the regime and the pervasive presence of the security services, Iraq is a particularly difficult HUMINT collection environment and the UN is unlikely to learn about its efforts to rebuild its nonconventional weapons programs. Without adequate intelligence, ongoing monitoring and verification efforts will face substantial obstacles. In addition, experience has shown that even the most effective monitoring and verification techniques available to the UN (such as on-site inspections, environmental sampling, and satellite and aerial surveillance) can be defeated by a resourceful adversary.

Finally, the success of the ongoing monitoring and verification effort is contingent on the unrestricted access of UN inspectors to Iraq. UN weapons inspections have been key to uncovering Iraq's nuclear, biological, chemical, and missile programs and in achieving what coalition airpower alone could not accomplish—the dismantling of Iraq's known nonconventional arsenal. For this reason, Iraq is not likely to accept the intrusive presence of inspectors indefinitely and might bar them at some future date. If this happens, it will become much more difficult to detect prohibited activities, since the direct detection techniques used by inspectors on the ground are inherently more sensitive and reliable than remote detection means. If Iraq were to ban inspectors from the country after replacing its inventory of dual-use equipment under the cover provided by UN resolutions, it could rebuild its nonconventional capabilities unhindered.

Sanctions and inspections are thus the most effective means to prevent Iraq from significantly augmenting its nonconventional capabilities—sanctions deny it the funds to undertake a major clandestine procurement effort, while inspections considerably constrain its activities. Together, they must remain the cornerstone of efforts to ensure that Iraq remains disarmed.

III   IRAQ'S CONVENTIONAL FORCES

On the eve of the Gulf War, Iraq had the largest armed forces in the Middle East, with about 750,000 men under arms. Its ground forces were organized into ten corps and sixty-seven divisions with 5,800 tanks, 5,100 APCs, and 3,850 artillery pieces.[1] Its air force had about 650 combat aircraft, and its navy had twenty-five surface combatants. In addition, Iraq's growing power-projection and long-range strike capabilities endowed it with the ability to influence events far from its borders and served as the basis for an increasingly activist regional policy.[2]

In the event of an Arab-Israeli war, Iraq could have contributed up to ten divisions to the effort, with the first elements arriving on its huge fleet of 2,800 tank transporters within the first three days of combat, and the rest arriving within two to three weeks.[3] In addition, its al-Husayn missiles and Su-24 and Mirage F-1E strike aircraft provided it with the

---

[1] These figures include large numbers of non-operational equipment kept in storage, and thus overstate Iraq's effective pre-war equipment inventory. Instead, the 3,475 tanks, 3,080 APCs, and 2,475 artillery pieces deployed in the Kuwaiti theatre during the Gulf War, provide a more accurate picture of the size of Iraq's effective inventory. *WP*, May 13, 1993, p. A6.

[2] Michael Eisenstadt, *"Sword of the Arabs:" Iraq's Strategic Weapons*, Policy Paper No. 21 (Washington, D.C.: The Washington Institute for Near East Policy, 1990), pp. 1-4, 41-59.

[3] DoD, *Conduct of the War*, p.9.

ability to deliver conventional and chemical payloads against civilian population centers throughout the region.[1]

The Gulf War struck a major blow to Iraqi regional ambitions. During the war it lost an estimated 2,633 tanks, 1,668 APCs, 2,196 artillery pieces, 300 aircraft, and twenty-five naval vessels, and while the number of soldiers killed and wounded was relatively small, 200,000-300,000 deserted or were taken prisoner.[2]

Since the war, Iraq has reorganized and downsized its armed forces. According to Defense Minister Gen. 'Ali Hasan al-Majid, Iraq's goal is to create a "small but strongly built army for two basic duties," that is, to "play a nationalistic role," and to "defend Iraq's security and borders" from Iraq's three main enemies: "Arab reactionary forces, Israel, and Iran."[3]

Iraq's armed forces are still the largest in the Gulf. The total strength of the Iraqi armed forces now stands at about 400,000 men. The ground forces have six corps with about thirty divisions, 2,200 tanks, 2,500 APCs, and 1,650 artillery pieces, and the air force has about 300 combat aircraft. The navy—for all intents and purposes—has ceased to exist.

While the armed forces have shown significant indications of recovery since the war—units have resumed regular operational and training activities, command and control has been restored, the military has been reorganized, and the logistical infrastructure has been repaired—there are also numerous signs of decline: much of its equipment is old and poorly maintained, severe deficiencies in the logistical

---

[1] Eisenstadt, *op cit.*, pp. 18-20, 24-28, 49-53.

[2] About 15,000-20,000 Iraqi soldiers were killed, 120,000-200,000 deserted, and 86,000 were taken prisoner during the Gulf War. Thousands more deserted during the uprising following the war and in subsequent fighting. *WP*, May 13, 1993, p. A6; Eliot A. Cohen and Thomas A. Keaney, *Gulf War Air Power Survey: Summary Report* (Washington, D.C.: Government Printing Office, 1993), p. 106; CIA, *Operation Desert Storm: A Snapshot of the Battlefield*, IA93-10022, September 1993; DoD, *Conduct of the War*, pp. 204, 206, 208, 411.

[3] *MEED*, January 17, 1992, p. 14.

system remain unresolved, readiness is affected by a lack of spares, and the military suffers from widespread demoralization.

Sanctions have had a critical impact on Iraq's conventional capabilities; they have prevented it from replacing its Gulf War losses, modernizing its aging equipment inventories, or acquiring repair parts for worn or damaged equipment.[1] The harmful impact of sanctions were acknowledged by Defense Minister Gen. 'Ali Hasan al-Majid in a recent interview in which he stated that sanctions are causing "known and important damage" to the armed forces and has forced it to use equipment previously "put out of service" as well as equipment "unfit for use" by other government agencies or civilians.[2]

Iraq has held contacts with Serbia, Slovakia, and the Ukraine, with the intent of concluding arms deals, although nothing is believed to have come of these meetings.[3] Moreover, it is believed to have achieved only a limited degree of success in smuggling weapons and spares for its military, including Bulgarian anti-tank and anti-aircraft weapons and large numbers of Chinese assault rifles;[4] the full dimensions of this trade, however, remain unknown.

---

[1] Resolution 687 states that "all states shall continue to prevent the sale or supply" of "conventional military equipment" of all types, "spare parts and components," and "technology used [in their] production" until further notice is given by the Security Council. UN, S/RES/687 (1991), April 3, 1991.

[2] Al-Thawra, January 6, 1993, p. 3, in FBIS-NES, January 8, 1993, p. 26. During a recent military parade in Baghdad intended to demonstrate the country's military might, several tanks broke down and had to be hauled off on tank transporters. LAT, June 15, 1993, p. A12.

[3] MEED, January 22, 1993, p. 11; LAT, June 15, 1993, p. A12.

[4] WT, August 18, 1992, p. 1; WT, September 8, 1992, p. 2. In one case that has come to light, seven Polish nationals were arrested in Germany in March 1992 while allegedly attempting to sell equipment worth DM160 million to Iraq, including two MiG aircraft, 4,000 mortars, and 80,000 AK assault rifles. Hamburg DPA, March 24, 1992, in FBIS-WEU, March 25, 1992, pp. 13-14.

TABLE 1

THE MILITARY BALANCE: IRAQ AND ITS NEIGHBORS

	Personnel	Divisions	Ind Bdes	Tanks	APCs	Artillery	Aircraft	Warships
Iraq	400,000	30	14	2,200	2,500	1,650	300	0
Iran	600,000	40	7	700	800	1,750	265	23
Saudi Arabia	100,000	-	15	700	3,000	700	275	24
Kuwait	10,000	-	2	100	150	25	60	1
Israel	500,000	12	13	3,850	8,100	1,300	550	24

Note: Except for Iraq, all these countries are involved in military expansion and modernization programs which could significantly enhance their capabilities in the coming years.
Source: MEMB: 1992-93 and other sources.

THE GROUND FORCES

Iraq's ground forces are the dominant arm of the military and consist of three main components: the Republican Guard; the regular army; and the popular militias.

• The Republican Guard is an elite corps-level formation that is independent of the army chain of command; it serves as the regime's principal offensive strike force and strategic reserve and has important internal security functions. Republican Guard units are better equipped and trained than regular army units and personnel (drawn largely from the Sunni Arab population) enjoy better pay and conditions of service than their regular army counterparts.

• The regular army is the largest component in the ground forces and is organized into a number of corps; each may control several armored, mechanized, and infantry divisions as well as several independent armored, infantry, artillery, special forces, and commando brigades and battalions.

• The popular militias include the Popular Army—the Ba'th party's 250,000 man militia—which by the late 1980s had an exclusively internal security function—and the National Defense Brigades—the 100,000 man pro-regime Kurdish militia—which fought against anti-regime Kurdish guerrillas during the Iran-Iraq War.

Iraq's ground forces now consist of six corps and thirty understrength divisions, with 2,200 tanks, 2,500 APCs, and 1,650 artillery pieces.[1] The ground forces were extensively reorganized after the Gulf War, building on the remnants of the Republican Guard and regular armored and mechanized divisions that survived the war, and elements of the ground forces that had remained outside of the theatre during the fighting.[2] The post-war reorganization of the ground forces

---

[1] DoD Regular Briefing, May 25, 1993. See also Appendix I.

[2] The post-war reorganization was facilitated by the fact that command and control of the ground forces had never been completely disrupted during the war. In a post-war speech Saddam claimed that despite more than forty days of bombing the "headquarters of corps, divisions, and

ended in late 1992—more than a year and a half after the war—when the army held its first post-war training exercise, marking the resumption of its annual training cycle.[1]

The army's current focus is on internal security and this is reflected in its current deployments:

• In the north, elements of three corps and sixteen divisions (including two Republican Guard and three heavy regular divisions), and more than 100,000 troops with 900 tanks, 1,000 APCs, and 1,000 artillery pieces face the Kurdish enclave.

• The Special Republican Guard and elements of several Republican Guard divisions with about 30,000 troops, 400 tanks, 500 APCs, and 200 artillery pieces are located in and around Baghdad and in the center of the country.

• In the south, elements of two corps, eight divisions (including one Republican Guard and three heavy regular divisions) and about 70,000 troops face Shi'i insurgents and civilians in the marshes.[2]

However, as a result of intensive efforts to repair the national communications system (rail lines, bridges, and telecommunications) since the war and the survival of most of the army's large inventory of tank transporters, the ground forces could rapidly redeploy to meet internal or external threats, and this pattern of deployments could quickly change.[3]

---

formations remained active until the last moment" as did the "chain of command" while "communications with these units was maintained." Radio Baghdad, March 2, 1992, in *FBIS-NES*, March 3, 1992, p. 37. A post-war air force assessment likewise concluded that "although the communications links between Baghdad and its field army...had been greatly reduced in capacity, sufficient 'connectivity' persisted for Baghdad to order a withdrawal from the theater that included some redeployments aimed at screening the retreat." *GWAPS, op cit.*, p. 70.

[1] *MEED*, November 13, 1992, p. 12.

[2] DoD Daily Briefing, May 25, 1993; *LAT*, August 2, 1992, p. A8; *JDW*, April 25, 1992, p. 687; *JDW*, August 8, 1992, p. 8.

[3] For more on the rebuilding of Iraq's transport and communications infrastructure see: *INA*, February 2, 1992, in *FBIS-NES*, February 4, 1993,

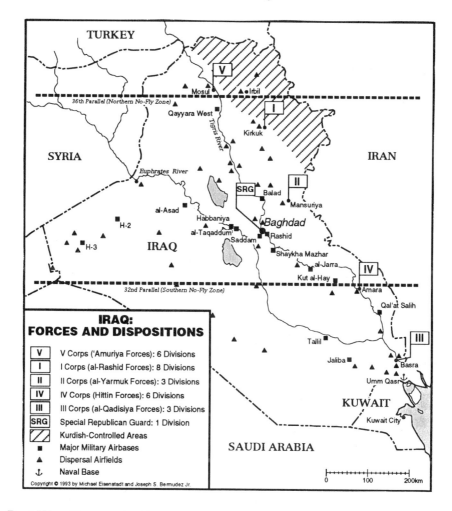

IRAQ: FORCES AND DISPOSITIONS

V	V Corps ('Amuriya Forces): 6 Divisions
I	I Corps (al-Rashid Forces): 8 Divisions
II	II Corps (al-Yarmuk Forces): 3 Divisions
IV	IV Corps (Hittin Forces): 6 Divisions
III	III Corps (al-Qadisiya Forces): 3 Divisions
SRG	Special Republican Guard: 1 Division
	Kurdish-Controlled Areas
■	Major Military Airbases
▲	Dispersal Airfields
⚓	Naval Base

Copyright © 1993 by Michael Eisenstadt and Joseph S. Bermudez Jr.

Post-War Reorganizations

Following the war, Iraq embarked on a far-reaching reorganization of its ground forces, involving the reconstitution of the Republican Guard and the regular armored and mechanized divisions, the disbanding of large numbers of regular infantry divisions, and the dissolution of the popular militias.

---

p. 22; *INA*, December 27, 1992, in *FBIS-NES*, December 30, 1992, p. 17. The national telephone system was the principal means of military communications at corps level and above, carrying more than half of all military communications. Its rapid repair thus has great military significance. DoD, *Conduct of the Persian Gulf Conflict (Interim Report)*, July 1991, pp. 2-4.

The Republican Guard emerged as the backbone of the ground forces; it was reorganized as a seven division corps and continues to serve as Baghdad's offensive strike force and strategic reserve. The continued importance of the Republican Guard derives in part from the fact that it proved to be the only force that consistently stood and fought coalition ground forces, that retained a significant combat capability, and that remained loyal to the regime after the war.[1] Significantly, it was the remnants of the Republican Guard's premier heavy divisions (the Tawakalna, Madina, and Hammurabi divisions—the same units which spearheaded the invasion of Kuwait), that led the effort to crush the uprising after the war. In addition, Republican Guard officers were transferred to regular army units following the war in order to raise combat standards in the regular army and ensure its loyalty.[2]

Iraq also disbanded a large number of regular army active and reserve infantry divisions and demobilized hundreds of thousands of soldiers assigned to these units during the war. Many of these infantry divisions offered little more than token resistance to coalition ground forces and suffered large numbers of desertions and prisoners taken; many, in fact, had ceased to exist as organized formations by the time of the cease-fire.

Finally, the regime disbanded the Popular Army and demobilized the National Defense Brigades after personnel from both organizations turned their guns on the regime during the uprising.[3] Recent reports indicate, however, that

---

[1] Despite efforts to target the Republican Guard for destruction, its losses were not as heavy as those suffered by regular army units during the war. According to post-war estimates the Republican Guard suffered only about 50 percent attrition for all major categories of weapons. By comparison, the attrition rate for regular army units in the theatre reached 75 percent for tanks, 50 percent for APCs, and 90 percent for artillery. CIA, *Operation Desert Storm*, September 1993.

[2] *WP*, March 30, 1991, pp. A1, A12.

[3] *INA*, April 26, 1991, in *FBIS-NES*, April 29, 1991, p. 11. Citizens were also called on to turn in any unauthorized weapons they might own. *AFP*, November 20, 1991, in *FBIS-NES*, November 21, 1991, p. 25.

Saddam has begun arming Kurdish and Shi'i tribesmen in order to restore government control to outlying areas.

The post-war reorganization of the armed forces has far-reaching domestic implications. The net effect of steps taken since the war—the reconstitution of the Republican Guard and the regular armored and mechanized divisions, the disbanding of large numbers of regular infantry divisions, and the dissolution of the popular militias—has been to strengthen the position of the regime and its most loyal forces *vis-à-vis* the regular army and the people, reducing the likelihood—at least for the near term—of a successful coup or uprising.

Equipment Inventories

Because Iraq committed its best units to combat during the Gulf War, it lost much of its most modern equipment in the fighting. It still has about 450 T-72 tanks, although most of its surviving equipment consists of older Soviet and Chinese Type 59, T-62, and Type 69 tanks, Type 63 APCs, and D-20, D-30, and M-46 towed artillery pieces.[1] Moreover, the Gulf War revealed critical shortcomings in nearly all of these key weapons systems.

The T-72M—Iraq's best tank—was shown to have inadequate armor protection and night vision capabilities,[2]

---

[1] House of Representatives Committee on Armed Services, *Intelligence Successes and Failures in Operations Desert Shield/Storm*, August 1993, pp. 30-32; CIA, *Operation Desert Storm*, September 1993. Some of the best equipment in Iraq's inventories are the 150 Chieftain tanks, 250 BMP-2 ICVs, and 50 M-901ITVs captured from Kuwait during the August 1990 invasion; according to UN Resolution 687 it is obliged to return these to the Kuwaitis. *Defense News*, February 24, 1992, pp. 1, 82.

[2] For instance, U.S. anti-armor penetrator rounds were able to destroy dug-in T-72s even after passing through 1.5 meter sand berms. Penetrations often resulted in catastrophic kills with the detonation of inadequately protected ammunition stores and the separation of turrets from hulls. In addition, the active infra-red night vision equipment on the T-72s was effective only at short ranges and ineffective during inclement weather. Ezio Bonsignore, "Gulf Experience Raises Tank Survivability Issues," *MT*, February 1992, pp. 64-70; Barbara Starr, "U.S. Armour Study Praises M1A1," *JDW*, August 24, 1991, p. 298.

while Iraq's much more numerous Type 59s, T-62s, and Type 69s suffer from even more serious shortcomings in the area of firepower, protection, and mobility.[1] Likewise, the Type 63 APC lacks adequate protection and armament, making it unsuitable for use as anything other than an armored transport. Most of Iraq's surviving artillery consists of a variety of older, less capable, and less survivable towed pieces, and the artillery corps continues to suffer from a number of problems: difficulties supporting such a diverse inventory of equipment, an inability to effectively employ target acquisition assets such as counterbattery radars, and a lack of ICMs and other modern munitions.[2]

Finally, deficiencies in the logistics system—particularly a shortage of wheeled transport[3]—limit Iraq's ability to support and sustain its ground forces in combat, while readiness has been affected by poor maintenance and a lack of spares. These factors significantly reduce Iraq's ability to project and sustain its forces or engage in high intensity combat, and would limit the scope and duration of any operation undertaken by the ground forces.

On the other hand, the army air corps emerged from the war relatively unscathed, with about 400 operational helicopters (including 150 attack helicopters)—a sizable force by any standard. Its Mi-8, Mi-25, and Bo-105 helicopters have played a major role in fighting against Kurdish and Shi'i insurgents following the war. Due to their numbers and their suitability for the counter-insurgency role, the army's helicopters are likely to play a central role in any future fighting involving the regime and its domestic foes.[4]

---

[1] See for instance: Stuart Slade, "Chinese Armoured Vehicles: You Get What You Pay For," *IDR*, January 1990, pp. 67-68.

[2] Captain Michael D. Holthus and Steven M. Chandler, "Myths and Lessons of Iraqi Artillery," *Field Artillery*, October 1991, pp. 7-9.

[3] More than half of all Iraqi trucks in the Kuwaiti theatre—which was a very large part of Iraq's total inventory—were destroyed during the Gulf War. GWAPS, *op cit.*, p. 97.

[4] Shlomo Gazit, ed., *Middle East Military Balance: 1992-93* (Israel: Tel Aviv University, Jaffee Center for Strategic Studies, 1993), p. 154.

AIR AND AIR DEFENSE FORCES

Before the Gulf War Iraq had the largest air force in the region, with about 650 combat aircraft, including several first-line aircraft—twenty-four Su-24s, twenty-four MiG-29s, and sixty-four Mirage F-1Es—and a much larger number of older and less capable Soviet and Chinese fighter and bomber aircraft. These aircraft were deployed to more than twenty-four main operating bases and thirty dispersal airfields throughout the country. Many of these airbases were built to world-class standards, featuring modern hardened aircraft shelters (built by British, Belgian, French, and Yugoslav contractors), multiple runways (connected by redundant taxiways), emergency operating surfaces, and well-developed support facilities.[1]

Due to its experience during the Iran-Iraq War, the Iraqi leadership had a limited appreciation of the potential of airpower prior to the Gulf War. In a revealing interview before the Gulf War, Saddam Hussein declared:

> Airpower has never decided a war in the history of wars. In the early days of the [Iran-Iraq War], the Iranians had an edge in the air... They flew to Baghdad like black clouds, but they did not determine the outcome of the battle. In later years, our air force gained supremacy, and yet it was not our air force that settled the war.[2]

Iraq's formidable air defenses were concentrated around major population and industrial centers and oriented to deal primarily with threats from Iran in the east and Israel in the west. The system was among the densest in the world, with more than 100 radar-guided SA-2/3/6/8 and Roland SAM batteries, 7,500 AAA guns, and 700 air defense radars.

The Baghdad air defense operations center (ADOC) was the heart of the system; it maintained the overall air picture and established air defense engagement priorities for the four

---

[1] Christopher M. Centner, "Ignorance is Risk: The Big Lesson from Desert Storm Air Base Attacks," *Airpower Journal*, Winter 1992, pp. 25-35.

[2] Radio Baghdad, August 30, 1990, in *FBIS-NES*, August 31, 1990, p. 22.

hardened sector operations centers (SOC), which controlled specific geographic areas of the country and numerous intercept operations centers (IOC) located in each sector. The ADOC, SOCs, IOCs, and numerous subordinate air defense radars, SAMs and AAA, and visual observers were linked into an integrated whole by the French-designed KARI air defense C3I system.

KARI provided a hardened, multi-layered, redundant, computer-controlled air defense capability. Extensively hardened facilities and secure land-line communications made the system very tough to shut down, while the use of automated data-integration and decision-making programs and redundant, high capacity communications provided it with some impressive battle management capabilities.[1]

The Air Force

Iraq currently has about 300 operational combat aircraft, although less than half can be considered modern types; these include about fifteen MiG-29s, thirty Mirage F-1s, fifty MiG-23s, thirty Su-20s, and twenty Su-25s. Moreover, the air force continues to suffer from a number of critical shortcomings: a shortage of aggressive and well-trained pilots;[2] a dearth of modern all-weather interceptors and strike aircraft; an inability to effectively coordinate air and ground components of its air defenses; excessive reliance on vulnerable ground-controlled intercept procedures; and problems ensuring adequate maintenance and spares.

During the war, Iraq sent all twenty-four of its Su-24s and twenty-four of its Mirage F-1Es—its most capable strike

---

[1] Rear Admiral Edward D. Sheafer, Director of Naval Intelligence, Statement before the Seapower, Strategic, and Critical Minerals Subcommittee of the House Armed Services Committee, February 5, 1992, p. 68; DoD, *Conduct of the War*, p. 12.

[2] Iraq's best (and only competent) pilots are considered to be from the group of fifty pilots that were trained in France on the Mirage F-1E during the mid-1980s. DoD, *Conduct of the War*, pp. 11-12; *GWAPS, op cit.*, pp. 125-126.

aircraft—to Iran for safekeeping.[1] Iran has since refused to return these aircraft. Thus Iraq lost the mainstay of its aerial long-range strike capability, and must now consider the threat these aircraft pose in Iranian hands.[2]

For more than a year after the Gulf War the Iraqi air force labored under the flight ban imposed by the coalition at the time of the cease-fire in March 1991. This ban placed severe constraints on Iraq's ability to train. Following an Iranian air strike on a Mojahedin-e Khalq base near Baghdad in April 1992, Iraq unilaterally resumed operational and training flights, although the northern and southern no-fly zones effectively restrict activities to the center of the country. Despite serious obstacles—its loss of access to foreign support services and sources of spares due to sanctions, and the serious damage suffered by its logistical support infrastructure during the Gulf War—the air force has succeeded in preserving a high level of readiness.[3] However, it is not clear that all 300 operational aircraft are fully mission-capable, or that its pilots have logged enough cockpit time to maintain anything more than a basic level of proficiency.

Iraq's air bases remain the strongest component of its air force. During the Gulf War, Iraq's air bases were targeted by coalition airpower in a concerted shelter-busting and runway cratering effort; 375 hardened shelters (of a total of 594) were destroyed or damaged while the air base support infrastructure (consisting of maintenance and logistics facilities) was heavily damaged.[4] Much of the damage has been repaired since the war; the Iraqis can probably shelter all of their operational aircraft at their thirty to forty operating air bases and dispersal airfields, while the rebuilt support infrastructure has been able to sustain a high level of operational activity.[5]

---

[1] The twenty-four Mirage F-1Es that Iraq sent to Iran comprised nearly its entire inventory of strike versions of this aircraft.

[2] For a breakdown of aircraft that fled to Iran by type, see Appendix I.

[3] This may be partly due to the contribution of idle maintenance personnel from Iraq's grounded state airline who are now employed by the air force.

[4] Centner, *op cit.*, pp. 25-35.

[5] *FT*, January 14, 1993, p. 4.

Air-Defense Forces

Although it took a pounding during the Gulf War, Iraq's air defense system remains largely intact: its major command and control centers (the ADOC and its subordinate SOCs and IOCs) survived heavy bombing and remain operational;[1] most of its SAMs and AAA survived the war since they were generally neutralized by non-destructive means (jamming and passive defensive measures); and sufficient numbers of air defense radars survived the war to provide countrywide coverage of Iraq's airspace without significant gaps.[2]

However, Iraq's air defenses continue to suffer from a number of major shortcomings, including: near total reliance on obsolete SAMs and AAA; less redundancy in its early warning radar coverage due to wartime losses; the loss of Soviet and French personnel critical to the operation of the system (particularly the integration of its Soviet and French radars, SAMs, computers, and electronics);[3] heavy reliance on less capable ground observers; and the demoralization which afflicts much of the military.

The condition of the air defenses is a source of particular concern for Iraq's senior leadership Thus in a March 1992 meeting, Saddam instructed his senior air defense commanders to emphasize "better tactical [and] technical deployment," the development of the "military personality" through "a higher level of training and exercises," and the

---

[1] According to one source, equipment and personnel were evacuated from various air defense command and control facilities during the war. *AW&ST*, January 27, 1992, p. 62. Thus, even though some of the buildings may have been heavily damaged by coalition bombing, the guts of the system survived, and the Iraqis were able to quickly rebuild them and return them to service.

[2] Of 700 stationary air defense radars, about 500 may have survived the war. Estimate based on figures in *GWAPS, op cit.*, pp. 229-230.

[3] About 200 Russian advisors reportedly remain in Iraq without official approval, however, and some of these continue to serve with the air defenses. Andrei Volpin, *Russian Arms Sales Policy Toward the Middle East,* Policy Focus No. 23 (Washington, D.C.: The Washington Institute for Near East Policy, 1993), p. 11.

restoration of "the fighters' morale...to the same level that they had enjoyed [before the war]."[1]

Several incidents since the war indicate, however, that the air and air defense forces continue to suffer from many problems:

• In April 1992, twelve Iranian aircraft raided Mojahedin-e Khalq bases located north of Baghdad. One airplane was lost to AAA fire. Iraqi aircraft, however, did not scramble to meet the enemy until after the raid, possibly indicating a failure of the air defense's early warning or command and control system.

• In December 1992, Iraq lost a MiG-25, and in January 1993, it lost a MiG-29 while challenging U.S. aircraft in the no-fly zones in northern and southern Iraq.

• In January 1993, coalition aircraft attacked the southern air defense sector SOC at Talil air base, killing a general and about thirty other officers in the process and damaging several IOCs and radar sites.[2]

• In May 1993, twelve Iranian air force aircraft again raided bases of the opposition Mojahedin-e Khalq organization, including one just northeast of Baghdad, without suffering any losses.

While the poor performance of Iraq's air and air defense forces against coalition aircraft since the war is not surprising given the qualitative disparities between the two sides, the fact that on two occasions Iranian aircraft have bombed targets near Baghdad (the most heavily defended part of the country) indicates that Iraq is unable to protect its airspace against even limited incursions by regional adversaries.

---

[1] Radio Baghdad, March 17, 1992, in *FBIS-NES*, March 18, 1992, p. 14.

[2] *WP*, January 23, 1993, p. A16.

NAVAL FORCES

Before the Gulf War the Iraqi navy was built around three principal components: 1) its maritime strike force, which consisted of Mirage F-1E strike aircraft and SA-321 Super Frelon helicopters armed with AM-39 Exocet anti-ship missiles; 2) its fleet of thirteen missile patrol boats, which included seven Osa-I/II, five ex-Kuwaiti TNC-45s, and one ex-Kuwait FPB-57; and 3) its coastal defense forces which consisted of several Silkworm missile batteries, its mine warfare forces (including nine minelayers and a very large number of naval mines of various types), and two marine brigades.

Iraq now has almost no naval or coastal defense forces left. It has perhaps a few SA-321 Super Frelon helicopters capable of carrying AM-39s, several small patrol boats, a small number of Silkworm coastal defense missiles, and some naval mines.[1] In addition, Italy has indicated that it would not deliver four Lupo-class frigates and four Asad-class missile corvettes it had built for Iraq.[2] As a result, there is little likelihood that Iraq will be able to modernize or rebuild its naval and coastal defense forces for some time to come.

With the limited naval assets at its disposal, Iraq's offensive options are restricted to hit-and-run attacks against lightly armed naval vessels or the harassment of unarmed merchant ships and fishing boats operating close to its shores. Moreover, it is capable of mounting little more than a token defense of its narrow coastline against the navies of Iran or other potential regional adversaries. It will be dependent on its air force to defend its coastline as long as the navy is incapable of doing so; however, the flight ban over southern Iraq will make it impossible for the air force to fulfill this role as long as the ban is in place. Consequently, its surviving inventory of Silkworm missiles and naval mines will comprise the mainstay of its coastal defenses for the foreseeable future.

---

[1] *MEMB*: 1992-93, *op cit.*, p. 264-265.
[2] *JDW*, March 21, 1992, p. 470; *JDW*, February 6, 1993, p. 10.

RESTORING MORALE: MISSION IMPOSSIBLE?

Except for the hard core Republican Guard and the army's better regular armored and mechanized divisions, the armed forces suffer from widespread demoralization due to the combined effects of the Gulf War defeat, war weariness (produced by a decade of fighting), and poor conditions of service as a result of sanctions. In addition to the nearly 200,000 soldiers who deserted or surrendered during the Gulf War, thousands joined the Kurdish and Shi'i rebels or deserted during the uprising, and thousands more deserted following several clashes since then. For instance, in July 1991, over 1,200 Iraqi soldiers surrendered to Kurdish *peshmerga* guerrillas after a series of clashes near Sulaymaniya, while in September 1991 nearly 800 soldiers surrendered after clashes near Kirkuk.[1] These episodes indicate that many soldiers in the regular army remain estranged from the regime, are unwilling to risk their lives in its defense, and continue to serve mainly to collect a pay check and receive perhaps two or three meager meals a day. They may also indicate that the various control mechanisms used to ensure discipline in the army remain weak or ineffective.

Saddam's decision in November 1991 to replace Defense Minister Lt. Gen. Husayn Kamil probably stemmed from the latter's failure to resolve the military's discipline and morale problems. His replacement by the thuggish 'Ali Hasan al-Majid, who earned a reputation for brutality while repressing insurgencies in Kurdistan in 1988 and Kuwait in 1990, was an indication of Saddam's distrust of the military and the magnitude of its morale problems. At the same time, Saddam also replaced the head of the MoD's political guidance directorate, Maj. Gen. Mundhir 'Abd-al-Rahman, for much the same reason.

Saddam has addressed the issue of morale in a number of speeches to his generals since the war, indicating that he considers it a significant problem. In one talk, Saddam lectured his commanders that "ideological building," which he

---

[1] *AFP*, July 21, 1991, in *FBIS-NES*, July 22, 1991, p. 15; *AFP*, September 16, 1991, in *FBIS-NES*, September 17, 1991, p. 20.

defined as "the building of faith and man and the awareness of and belief in the message" is not just "a matter for the Moral Guidance Directorate," but rather "the concern of all of you."[1] In another talk, Saddam explained to his commanders that a military "does not fight only with its weapons" but also with "its moral and spiritual structure, based on conviction." The commanders, he continued, "are the ones who implant" in the soldiers "the example to which they should look under all circumstances." Thus, when they see that their commander "is shaken by a difficult situation, it affects them." Consequently, the commander should "reassure them." To do so, he continued, will require the commanders to "make the military everything" in their life which is "no longer...easy."[2]

There are other signs of trouble as well. The Revolution Command Council—the regime's supreme decision-making body—recently decreed that military personnel who fail to maintain proper "military discipline and control" as well as "military honor" will be discharged with a reduction in rank (thereby reducing their pension entitlement), while servicemen who choose to resign or retire at their own request will suffer the loss of certain retirement benefits.[3] In addition, the regime has repeatedly extended amnesty offers to deserters, indicating that desertion is still a problem.[4] Finally, many who are eligible to serve refuse to report for duty.[5]

---

[1] Radio Baghdad, December 14, 1991, in *FBIS-NES*, December 16, 1991, p. 39.

[2] Radio Baghdad, January 13, 1992, in *FBIS-NES*, January 15, 1991, pp. 24-25.

[3] *Al-Thawra*, March 15, 1992, p. 1, in *FBIS-NES*, March 20, 1992, pp. 16-17; *Babil*, November 22, 1992, p. 1, in *FBIS-NES*, December 1, 1992, p. 24.

[4] Radio Baghdad, May 8, 1991, in *FBIS-NES*, May 9, 1991, p. 14; INA, July 21, 1991 in *FBIS-NES*, July 22, 1991, p. 12; Radio Baghdad, December 19, 1991, in *FBIS-NES*, December 20, 1991, p. 20; Radio Baghdad, September 6, 1992, in *FBIS-NES*, September 8, 1992, p. 30; Radio Baghdad, September 17, 1992, in *FBIS-NES*, September 17, 1992, p. 18; Radio Baghdad, September 20, 1992, in *FBIS-NES*, September 23, 1992, p. 23.

[5] For instance, a call-up of new eighteen year-old conscripts in July 1992 included a call to "draft dodgers and those who no longer have excuses [to defer their military service]." Radio Baghdad, July 28, 1992, in *FBIS-NES*, July 29, 1992, p. 25.

Saddam has attempted to rectify these problems by improving conditions of service and offering various blandishments to the military. These include:

• Increasing military salaries several-fold since the war through a series of raises, while granting cash bonuses and other benefits, such as land grants, housing and other loans, and cars to soldiers who continue to serve.[1]

• Reducing the term of compulsory service—thirty-six months for most draftees—to eighteen months for college graduates, and four months for advanced degree holders, while permitting the latter to serve part of their time in civilian ministries.[2]

• Permitting automatic retirement for officers and senior enlisted personnel who have served for twenty-five years or more. Previously, special permission was required.[3]

All available evidence, however, indicates that Saddam's efforts to restore the self-confidence, discipline, and morale of his war-weary military have not succeeded. Moreover, they are not likely to do so as long as sanctions—which have created general conditions of hardship in Iraq and difficult conditions of service in the military—remain in place.

---

[1] Radio Monte Carlo, July 30, 1991, in *FBIS-NES*, July 31, 1991, p. 21; *INA*, September 5, 1991, in *FBIS-NES*, September 6, 1991, p. 7; Radio Baghdad, September 8, 1991, in *FBIS-NES*, September 9, 1991, p. 15; *al-Thawra*, September 16, 1991, p. 1, in *FBIS-NES*, September 19, 1991, p. 15; Radio Baghdad, October 3, 1991, in *FBIS-NES*, October 4, 1991, p. 12.

[2] These steps may have also been motivated by a desire to encourage the civilian reconstruction effort and to placate the politically important middle class. *Babil*, August 29, 1991, p. 1, in *FBIS-NES*, September 3, 1991, pp. 31-32; Radio Baghdad, December 8, 1991, in *FBIS-NES*, December 10, 1991, p. 38; Radio Baghdad, December 19, 1991, in *FBIS-NES*, December 20, 1991, pp. 20-21; *INA*, February 20, 1992, in *FBIS-NES*, February 24, 1992, p. 44.

[3] *MEED*, May 31, 1991, p. 22.

MILITARY PRODUCTION CAPABILITIES

Before the Gulf War, Iraq's military industries were involved in a wide range of activities: the development and production of nuclear, biological, and chemical weapons and ballistic missiles, the assembly of T-72 tanks, the modification and repair of aircraft, tanks, and other armored vehicles, and the production of bombs, tube and rocket artillery, naval mines, small arms, small boats, and ammunition.[1] A significant part of Iraq's industrial base was dedicated to this effort, and because some industrial facilities were involved in both military and civilian production, the distinction between the two sectors was often blurred.[2] As a result, many civilian industrial facilities will have to be monitored in order to prevent Iraq from rebuilding its nonconventional military capabilities. This has led Iraqi officials to charge that UN efforts to monitor its civilian industries are in fact motivated by a desire to thwart its economic development.

With all that it invested in creating a modern military-industrial infrastructure, Iraq lacked the skilled manpower base required to support this effort.[3] The largest pool of talented managers, scientists, and technicians were employed in the nuclear program, which was the regime's number one priority. This left Iraq's other weapons programs with only a small number of qualified and experienced people to fill the top positions; at lower levels there was often a void of skills and experience. Thus, UN inspectors have noted that when sophisticated machinery employed by Iraq's chemical weapon program broke down, it often remained idle for long periods until it was repaired or discarded, thereby reducing

---

[1] See Appendix V.

[2] For instance, the al-Amin (*'Uqba bin Nafi'*) workshop at Batra was engaged in the assembly of precision machine tools, the maintenance of T-72 tanks (as well as the production of spare parts for the T-72), and the manufacture of parts for hydroelectric power stations. IAEA-11, S/23947, May 22, 1992, p. 24.

[3] David Isby, "Electronic Warfare in the Gulf War," unpublished paper, p. 3.

productivity.[1] Similar observations have been made concerning Iraq's missile program.[2]

Since the war, Iraq has devoted significant resources—despite severe financial and material constraints—to rebuilding its conventional military-industrial infrastructure. Although many military-industrial installations were heavily damaged during the war, reconstruction has proceeded rapidly. In many cases reconstruction was expedited by the fact that hard-to-replace equipment and machine tools were removed from factories prior to the bombing, or were salvaged from the rubble.[3] Significant reconstruction has been reported at more than two dozen military-industrial sites; more than 200 buildings have been restored and many more are in the process of being repaired.[4] Iraq has reportedly resumed assembly of T-72 tanks (from unassembled kits remaining from before the war) and limited production of artillery, short-range missiles and rockets (which it is permitted to produce under the terms of the cease-fire), ammunition, small arms, and spares. Production remains far below pre-war levels, however, and is likely to do so as long as sanctions continue to restrict access to raw materials and repair parts for damaged machinery.[5]

---

[1] Steven Mataija and J. Marshall Beier (Eds.), *Multilateral Verification and the Post-Gulf Environment: Learning from the UNSCOM Experience* (York University: Centre for International and Strategic Studies, December 1992), p. 119.

[2] William Lowther, *Arms and the Man: Gerald Bull, Iraq, and the Supergun* (New York: Ivy Books, 1991), p. 207.

[3] See Appendix IV.

[4] Robert Gates, Director of the Central Intelligence Agency, Statement before the U.S. House of Representatives Armed Services Committee Defense Policy Panel, March 27, 1992, p. 8. According to Iraqi sources, as of January 1992, 187 destroyed or damaged military-industrial buildings had been repaired and another 260 were undergoing repair. Bernd Debusmann, "Postwar Iraq Rebuilds Rapidly," *WT*, January 12, 1992, p. 14.

[5] General Joseph Hoar, Central Command 1993 Posture Statement, p. 21; Gates, *op cit.*, p. 8.

CONCLUSIONS

The post-war reorganization of the armed forces served to strengthen the domestic position of the regime. The only units capable of undertaking a coup—the Special Republican Guard and the Republican Guard—have proven to be largely loyal. By contrast, the regular army remains, for the most part, weak and demoralized, and incapable of a coup. Moreover, the extraordinary security around Saddam would make a coup very difficult, although his demise at the hands of an assassin or a disgruntled bodyguard cannot be ruled out. Finally, the civilian population—which is crushed, disarmed, and utterly demoralized—is unlikely to rise in revolt again.

Iraq still has the largest armed forces in the Gulf, and if revitalized, they could once again emerge as a force of instability in the region. For now, however, Iraq's ability to threaten its larger neighbors—like Iran or Saudi Arabia—is limited due to its uncertain domestic situation and the significant shortcomings of its ground forces; these include obsolete and poorly maintained equipment, deficiencies in its logistical system (particularly a shortage of wheeled transport) which limit its ability to support and sustain its forces in combat, a shortage of spare parts, and low morale—which would produce massive desertions in the event of combat. Iraq's air force could not make a significant contribution to any effort due to its own inherent shortcomings as well as the presence of no-fly zones in northern and southern Iraq which limit its freedom of action, while the navy would be limited to small hit-and-run attacks against lightly armed naval vessels or unarmed merchant ships close to its shores.

As long as sanctions remain in place, Iraq will be unable to rebuild its conventional forces or rectify its most pressing problems—the need to replace Gulf War losses, modernize its aging inventory of arms, acquire repair parts for damaged or worn equipment, and improve conditions of service in order to raise morale—and its military capabilities will remain limited.

Iraq nonetheless remains a potential troublemaker since, as shown by recent events, it could draw U.S. forces into combat if it were to invade or threaten Kuwait, attempt to retake the Kurdish enclave in the north of the country, challenge the northern or southern no-fly zones, or sponsor acts of terror.

IV   SADDAM'S MILITARY OPTIONS

There are a number of places where Iraq could—in the future—resort to force to achieve key objectives: 1) the Kurdish enclave; 2) Kuwait; and 3) the northern and southern no-fly zones. In addition, Iraq's border with Iran is likely to remain a potential flash-point in the future. Contingencies for each of these areas are examined in detail below.

SADDAM'S POISED HAMMER: THE MILITARY THREAT TO THE KURDS

One of Saddam's chief policy objectives is regaining control of the Kurdish north. As long as the north remains out of his hands, it will be a focus of opposition activity and potential foreign military intervention. By massing forces along the borders of Kurdistan, crippling the Kurdish economy by an embargo, and launching terrorist attacks against relief convoys and foreign aid workers, Saddam hopes to bring the Kurds to their knees and force them to come to terms with him. In this way, Saddam hopes not only to regain control of the north without triggering foreign intervention, but also to split the Kurds from the Iraqi National Congress, and thereby break the back of the opposition.[1]

---

[1] For instance, a recent article in *al-Thawra* advised the Kurds that "the road to Baghdad is the only safe, open road" that will "save the autonomous region" since "betting on the foreigners is not wise" and "only reflects bankruptcy." The article went on to remind the Kurds that "Iraq will remain" and "Saddam Husayn will remain" and that "he is

Saddam is likely to bide his time in the hope that the embargo and a growing sense of abandonment will force the Kurds into submission; in the meantime he is focusing on the Shi'i opposition in the south, which he considers a more immediate threat. Ground operations against Shi'i insurgents continue despite the imposition of the no-fly zone there. As a result of the recent completion of three man-made rivers (the Saddam, Qadisiya, and Umm al-Ma'arik) which are draining the vast marshes that provide refuge to the insurgents, and the forced resettlement or flight of thousands of civilians who provide them with food and shelter, the resistance in the south is likely to lose much of its strength in the coming year.[1]

It is possible, however, that Saddam would attempt to retake the north by force if he believed that there were little likelihood of a military response by coalition forces, particularly if the United States were distracted by a crisis elsewhere in the world. Nearly two-thirds of the Iraqi army—including some of its best units—are deployed facing the Kurds in the north; these forces enjoy a broad margin of superiority over the lightly-armed Kurdish *peshmerga* guerrillas and are kept on a footing that would enable them to initiate operations against the Kurdish enclave with very short notice.

Any Iraqi attempt to retake the north would hinge on two factors—achieving surprise and preventing foreign military intervention. Saddam might believe that by quickly retaking the north or parts of it and blocking the mass flight to Turkey of hundreds of thousands of Kurds, he could present the world with a *fait accompli* and minimize the risk of outside intervention.

Accordingly, an Iraqi attempt to retake the north would commence with the insertion of helicopter-borne troops in major mountain passes and river valleys along the Turkish border to prevent Kurdish civilians from fleeing to Turkey.

---

the only guarantee for both the Kurds and the Arabs." *INA*, May 28, 1993, in *FBIS-NES*, May 28, 1993, p. 16.

[1] Max van der Stoel, "The Situation of Human Rights in Iraq," U.N. Economic and Social Council, February 19, 1993, pp. 35-40.

With the benefit of surprise, Iraqi transport helicopters could accomplish their mission before coalition aircraft could respond. Meanwhile, Republican Guard and regular armored and mechanized divisions would dash to the border to link up with these forces and seal the frontier. Moving quickly to crush any resistance in the major urban centers, they would use artillery to pound the Kurds into submission. The numerous low grade infantry divisions would be used for less demanding roles, such as securing lines of communication and maintaining order in pacified areas. This would minimize the possibility of large-scale desertions from these units.

At present, Iraq's armed forces are incapable of conducting this kind of fast-paced, combined arms operation requiring the coordination of large forces over large areas. Moreover, its forces are unlikely to succeed in completely subduing Kurdish guerrillas in the mountainous areas and would be dependent on long supply lines that could be interdicted by the guerrillas. Consequently, Baghdad has to consider the possibility that an attempt to quickly retake the north could bog down into a protracted war of attrition against tenacious guerrilla fighters in difficult terrain. Finally, Iraqi forces would probably suffer massive desertions that could make it difficult to maintain their hold on territory retaken from the Kurds.

Saddam could, however, cut his risks by limiting initial efforts at retaking only the eastern part of the Kurdish enclave below the 36th parallel. A limited thrust would have a greater chance of success and reduce the likelihood of foreign intervention since most of the Kurds who would flee would probably go to Iran or other parts of the enclave.

Iraq must also consider the potential impact of coalition military intervention. Coalition forces in the theatre include about one hundred combat aircraft based in Turkey (not all of which have a ground attack capability), which could be augmented by another sixty combat aircraft in Saudi Arabia and elements of at least one aircraft carrier air wing (fifty to sixty combat aircraft) from a carrier in the eastern Mediterranean or Arabian Sea. These air assets could generate up to 300 ground attack sorties per day, and could dramatically raise the cost of Iraqi aggression, strengthen Kurdish resolve, and prompt widespread desertions by Iraqi troops. Despite the small size of available coalition air assets, they could make any Iraqi attempt to retake the north very costly.

An attempt by Iraq to retake the Kurdish enclave is thus not likely at this time, although this assessment could change if the United States were to become engaged in major military commitments elsewhere in the world or if the U.S. commitment to protect the Kurds appeared to be waning.

"IRAQ'S 19TH PROVINCE": THE ABIDING MILITARY THREAT TO KUWAIT

Iraq remains committed to the restoration of its sovereignty over Kuwait (at least on the level of its declaratory policy),[1] and given the opportunity, it could again invade the emirate. Iraq's ground forces still enjoy overwhelming superiority over Kuwait's 10,000 man army and could—even now—retake the country in relatively short order. However, Iraq remains deterred by the prospect of another war with the United States and its coalition partners, and it is unlikely to act while most of its forces are engaged in internal security operations in the north and south of the country. Thus, under present circumstances, Iraq does not pose an immediate military threat to Kuwait. And because most of its army (including many of its best units) are in the north facing the Kurds while other units in the south are tied down fighting the 10,000 Shi'i insurgents in the marshes, a large number of units would have to be redeployed from the north to the south before it could pose a threat, providing advanced warning of its intentions.

---

[1] For instance, Oil Minister Usama 'Abd al-Razzaq al-Hitti recently asserted that "Historically, we have a right to Kuwait. It was carved up unjustly and aggressively." *Al-Jumhuriya*, June 2, 1993, p. 2, in *FBIS-NES*, June 7, 1993, p. 30. Likewise, on the third anniversary of the invasion of Kuwait, the daily newspaper *Babil*, published by Saddam's son 'Uday said that Iraqis constantly discuss "the severance of Kuwait from Iraq and look for the day it will be returned." *WT*, August 3, 1993, p. A7. Similarly, on the third anniversary of the annexation of Kuwait, the daily newspaper *al-Jumhuriya* stressed that the annexation decree "will remain a historic one for generations to come because it stresses a historical fact that force cannot change or cancel." *Al-Jumhuriya*, August 7, 1993.

Should Saddam attempt to retake Kuwait once again, he is likely to proceed with a number of Gulf War lessons in mind. In a meeting with Ba'th party members in Basra after the war, Saddam reportedly acknowledged that he had made a number of mistakes.[1] These included:

• Not continuing the attack into Saudi Arabia's oil-rich eastern province and mining the oil fields there. He could have then used his control over most of the world's oil and the threat of setting the fields ablaze as a bargaining chip, offering to trade them for Kuwait.

• Releasing the Western hostages held by Iraq before the war, in the belief that this step would placate the Europeans and undermine the coalition.

• Not attacking U.S. troops when they first arrived in the region before a coalition could be formed and additional reinforcements sent. Had he done so, he would have met with military success, creating pressure for the United States to cut its losses, withdraw, and leave him with Kuwait.

While Iraq could invade Kuwait again, its ability to project and sustain forces all the way to the oil fields and port facilities in eastern Saudi Arabia are far beyond its current capabilities and will remain so for some time to come.

Although Iraq remains a long-term threat to Kuwait, it is unlikely to implement its threats against the tiny emirate as long as the U.S. deterrent remains strong and credible. Thus, lacking an immediate military option against Kuwait, Baghdad is likely to continue its threats against the country and its ruling family, while sponsoring terrorist attacks and abducting and harassing foreign workers in disputed border areas.

---

[1] As reported by opposition sources. See, Voice of the Iraqi People, March 24, 1992, in *FBIS-NES*, March 25, 1992, p. 18.

CHALLENGING THE NO-FLY ZONES

Iraqi officials have said that they consider the northern and southern no-fly zones as a violation of the territorial integrity of Iraq. They are thus committed to work for their removal as part of their efforts to restore Iraqi sovereignty throughout their country and to increase their political and military freedom of action.[1]

Iraq is working to undermine the no-fly zones primarily by indirect means. In the north, it is using military threats, an economic embargo, and terrorism to force the Kurds to reconcile with the regime. In the south, it is using military action on the ground, the uprooting of the civilian population, and the desiccation of the marshes, to bring about the collapse of the opposition there. The regime apparently hopes that success on the ground will eventually undermine the rationale for the no-fly zones.

Iraq has also challenged the no-fly zones by direct means —engaging coalition aircraft in air-to-air combat or by SAM and AAA fire—in the hope of downing an aircraft or capturing a pilot, thereby scoring a military victory and providing the regime with political leverage over the coalition. Iraq has also harassed coalition aircraft by illuminating them with air defense tracking radars in order to provoke an attack on its air defenses; these incidents may be initiated for domestic reasons—to enable the regime to portray Iraq as the victim of unwarranted foreign aggression and thereby redirect popular discontent toward its foreign enemies. Iraq is thus again likely to challenge coalition aircraft patrolling the no-fly

---

[1] For instance, according to Vice President Taha Yassin Ramadan, "Even while saying they were opposed to fragmenting Iraq, the coalition countries, the United States, Britain, and France, announced the partition of Iraq in accordance with lines of latitude and longitude and declared that Iraqi planes were forbidden to fly... [thereby] implementing a partition on ugly ethnic and sectarian foundations.... We reject it. Our rejection is not merely implied.... We said we will confront it at a time and place of our choosing and in an appropriate way." *Al-Sha'b*, January 26, 1993, p. 3, in *FBIS-NES*, February 1, 1993, p. 27.

zones, in the hope of gaining tactical advantage over the coalition and enhancing the domestic standing of the regime.

IRAN: CONFLICT OR COOPERATION?

Iraq and Iran remain bitter enemies. Because both countries seek hegemony in the Gulf, and because many of the issues that have led to conflict in the past remain unresolved, future relations between the two countries are more likely to be characterized by conflict and competition than by cooperation. Iraq is unlikely to attack or provoke Iran, however, as long as its armed forces remain weakened by war and sanctions.

However, the U.S. declaration of a policy of "dual containment" toward Iraq and Iran[1] has fed speculation that common interests and circumstances might prompt the two countries to work together to thwart U.S. aims and that cooperation might even include activities in the military sphere.[2] There are in fact a number of precedents for such a scenario.

Several months before Iraq invaded Kuwait in August 1990, it proposed a "strategic alliance" with Iran as part of its effort to form a new regional alignment to counter U.S. power and influence in the region, expand Iraqi influence in the Gulf, and confront Israel.[3] While these efforts to forge a new regional alignment failed, they did result in a series of agreements between Iraq and Iran that were signed in January

---

[1] For more on "dual containment," see: Martin Indyk, "Clinton Administration Policy Toward the Middle East," Soref Symposium Proceedings, The Washington Institute for Near East Policy, May 18, 1993.

[2] *WP*, May 23, 1993, p. A26; *WP*, July 1, 1993, p. A18.

[3] Ofra Bengio, "Iraq," in *Middle East Contemporary Survey* (New York: Holmes and Meier, 1990), pp. 395-397, 409-410. This was not the first time that Iraq tried to forge an alliance with Iran to confront their mutual enemies and extricate itself from a difficult situation. In June 1982, at the height of its war with Iran, Iraq announced a unilateral cease-fire and urged the creation of a new anti-Israel bloc spearheaded by Iraq and incorporating Iran in order to confront Israel following its invasion of Lebanon. Ofra Bengio, "Iraq," in *MECS, op cit.,* 1981-82, pp. 582, 585.

1991—just a few days before the Gulf War—concerning cooperation between the two countries during the impending conflict. As part of this agreement, Iran agreed to provide safehaven to thirty-three Iraqi civilian passenger and transport aircraft which arrived on the eve of the war.

Additional agreements were concluded concerning the provision of refuge for Iraqi ships in Iranian territorial waters, granting access to Iranian satellite ground station and telecommunications services, the use of Iranian airspace, and the transshipment of oil through Iranian ports. There is no evidence, however, that any of these additional agreements were implemented.

During the war, Iraq dispatched over 115 combat aircraft (including some of its best fighters) and eleven naval vessels to Iran; nearly all the aircraft and two of the ships survived the trip. These movements—which were apparently not covered by any pre-war agreements—came as a surprise to the Iranians.[1] Iraq had apparently hoped that Iran would permit it to use these assets later in the war to bloody the United States; on this count it appears to have miscalculated. Both the aircraft and the naval vessels remain in Iran to this day.

Moreover, in recent months there have been reports that Iraq has bartered quantities of oil, steel, and possibly cement and fertilizers to Iran in return for foodstuffs and spare parts. This trade permits Iraq to reduce the impact of sanctions and acquire vital supplies.[2]

Past experience thus shows that economic cooperation between Iran and Iraq is much more likely than cooperation in the military sphere, although military cooperation between the two countries cannot be ruled out. The potential for cooperation will, however, be limited by the fact that both Iran and Iraq are pursuing fundamentally incompatible regional

---

[1] Mohamed Heikal, *Illusions of Triumph: An Arab View of the Gulf War* (N.Y.: HarperCollins Publishers, 1992), pp. 303-304; DoD, *Conduct of the War*, pp. 129, 195.

[2] *WP*, March 28, 1993, p. A1; *WP*, May 23, 1993, p. A26; *WP*, July 1, 1993, p. A18.

objectives, by Iran's desire that any assistance not significantly enhance Iraq's military capabilities or tip the military balance in its favor, and by the mutual distrust which characterizes the relationship between the two countries.

Because it is in Iran's interest to weaken both the United States and Iraq without exposing itself to retribution by either side, Iran is not likely to openly join Iraq in confronting the United States or to openly assist it (although before the Gulf War some in Iran called for an open alliance with Iraq against the United States and the coalition). Rather, Iran is likely to limit itself to quietly helping Iraq confront the United States by: 1) assisting Iraqi air defenses to locate and identify U.S. combat air patrols and incoming strike packages; 2) providing combat intelligence; and 3) providing target data that could be used to plan attacks against U.S. warships in the Gulf. While such assistance could conceivably complicate U.S. military operations or planning against Iraq, it is not likely to have a decisive impact on the outcome of any future conflict or significantly enhance Iraqi military capabilities.

V CONCLUSIONS

Although currently weak and isolated, the regime of President Saddam Hussein remains committed to making Iraq a regional power and rebuilding its military capabilities, and therefore it will continue to pose a threat to regional peace and stability. Consequently, Iraq will remain a threat to U.S. interests in the Middle East for the foreseeable future. Even now, despite restrictive sanctions and intrusive inspections, there are indications that Iraq may be planning to resurrect its nuclear program, and that it retains a residual biological and chemical warfare capability. Iraq's abiding interest in acquiring nonconventional weapons and rebuilding its conventional forces will be among the most critical challenges facing the United States in the Middle East in the coming years.

If sanctions and inspections were to cease, Iraq could rebuild its nonconventional capabilities in less time, with a smaller investment of resources, personnel, and money than it would take to restore its conventional capabilities. Iraq could probably produce nuclear weapons within five to seven years (much sooner if it were to acquire fissile material from abroad), restore its former chemical weapons production capability in less than one year, and produce militarily significant quantities of biological weapons within weeks (if it cannot already do so); this could cost a few million to a few billion dollars, depending on the nature and scope of the effort. By contrast, it could take five to eight years and many billions of dollars to restore its conventional capabilities.

In light of this assessment, United States policy should actively seek the overthrow of Saddam Hussein and his regime, while aiming to contain Iraq by three principal means: maintaining sanctions, retaining a forward military presence in the region, and preserving the Gulf War coalition.

Maintaining Sanctions

Sanctions have thus far been extremely effective in preventing Baghdad from restoring its military capabilities. Their impact has been manifest on several levels: The ban on the sale of oil (which could bring Iraq an estimated $12-15 billion a year) has been crucial in denying Iraq the funds that would enable it to once again engage in the large-scale smuggling of dual-use equipment and technology. The ban on arms transfers has prevented Iraq from restoring its conventional military capabilities by replacing its Gulf War losses, modernizing its aging inventory of arms, or acquiring repair parts for damaged equipment. And the general atmosphere of hardship and privation in Iraq caused, in part, by sanctions has contributed to the widespread demoralization of the armed forces. This is a major constraint on the regime's military freedom of action. Consequently, the United States must do all it can to ensure that all the components of sanctions—the ban on Iraqi oil sales, exports to Iraq, and arms transfers—remain in place as long as the current regime in Baghdad remains in power.

The United States is likely to face a test of its political resolve on the issue of sanctions in the near future. Iraq has been engaged in political consultations with France and Russia on the lifting of sanctions and took a number of steps during recent meetings with UNSCOM toward compliance with the parts of Resolution 687 pertaining to the dismantling of its nonconventional weapons programs. However, if the ban on oil sales is lifted as 687 mandates, Iraq will once again have billions of dollars at its disposal. Washington must do whatever is necessary—including vetoing attempts in the Security Council to lift sanctions—to avert this eventuality, even if that means, in effect, changing the rules in mid-game. While several countries—particularly France and Russia—are likely to oppose such efforts by the United States to block the lifting of sanctions, the United States will have to explain to its allies that this issue affects vital U.S. interests and the peace and stability of this crucial region, and that the violation of the sanctions by these countries would have serious implications for their relations with the U.S.

Retaining a Forward Military Presence

The United States' forward military presence in the region—specifically the composite air wings at Incirlik, Turkey and Dharan, Saudi Arabia, respectively—are vital to U.S. efforts to deter renewed Iraqi aggression against Kuwait and the Kurdish enclave in northern Iraq. Airpower offers the United States a degree of responsiveness and flexibility in dealing with the Iraqi threat that is not offered by other options (such as the prepositioning of U.S. armor in the region), and is a tangible demonstration of the U.S. commitment to safeguard Kuwait and the Kurds. This forward presence also reduces Saddam's freedom of maneuver, since the coalition can respond immediately to aggression or provocations. Without such a forward presence Saddam might be tempted to test U.S. resolve. This forward presence must, however, be periodically buttressed by authoritative and clear statements reaffirming the U.S. commitment to respond to Iraqi aggression and safeguard the independence and territorial integrity of Kuwait, and the welfare of the Kurds in the enclave in northern Iraq.

The United States must also maintain the northern and southern no-fly zones. While the no-fly zones do not significantly constrain Iraq on the ground, they serve a useful purpose. Since SAMs are not permitted in the no-fly zones, coalition air assets would face a reduced air defense threat should they be required to intervene there. Maintaining the no-fly zones is also a significant public demonstration of Washington's resolve.

Preserving the Coalition

It is vital to maintain a coalition of states—the most important being France, Russia, Turkey, Saudi Arabia, and Jordan—which are committed to preventing Iraq from rebuilding its military capabilities. France and Russia are particularly important since they were major arms suppliers and trade partners with Baghdad before the Gulf War and stand to gain a great deal if sanctions are raised—particularly since Iraq remains the largest untapped arms market in the world today. Turkey and Saudi Arabia are important because U.S. aircraft are based there and their assent would be required for military action involving these aircraft. Finally, Turkey and Jordan are crucial for ensuring the effectiveness of sanctions, since these two countries are major routes for smuggling into Iraq. The United States may have to expend significant political capital in the future in order to maintain the coalition and keep potential weak links such as France, Russia, and Turkey on board, and with the passage of time it is likely to become more difficult to maintain broad international support for sanctions. However, because of the stakes involved, the United States has no choice but to use its considerable influence to ensure that sanctions remain in place for as long as necessary.

Because Iraq has traditionally played a role in both the Arab-Israeli and Persian Gulf arenas, the potential costs of failing to prevent its rearmament are very high. There can be little doubt that a rearmed Iraq would pose a threat to regional peace and stability. It would resume its quest for regional hegemony, seek to avenge its defeat at the hands of the United States and its coalition partners, and work to undermine U.S. interests in the region by disrupting the Arab-Israeli peace process (which it opposes) and supporting radical and rejectionist forces. Strapped by massive debts and driven by unrequited ambitions, the economic pressures which led Iraq to invade Kuwait in 1990 could once again lead it to cast a covetous eye on its more wealthy but less powerful neighbors, perhaps spurring new military aggression and again threatening the flow of oil from the region. Finally, a failure to implement Resolution 687 will doom arms control efforts in the Middle East; no country in the region will be willing to cut their forces as long as Iraq remains a threat. For these reasons, the containment of Iraq—through deterrence and sanctions— must remain a cornerstone of U.S. policy in the Middle East as long as the current regime in Baghdad remains in power.

APPENDICES

APPENDIX I

IRAQ: GULF WAR LOSSES AND CURRENT STRENGTH

	Men	Tanks	APCs	Artillery	Aircraft	Naval Craft
Pre-War Totals:	750,000	5,800	5,100	3,850	650	25
Forces in Kuwaiti Theatre:	420,000	3,475	3,080	2,475	----	25
Losses:	15,000	2,633	1,668	2,196	350	25
Current Strength:	400,000	2,200	2,500	1,650	300	0

Notes:

1. Pre-war equipment totals significantly overstate Iraqi military strength on the eve of the war, and include many pieces of equipment that were in storage or non-operational. Consequently, there are discrepancies between pre-war totals, wartime losses, and current strength figures (the latter does not include non-operational items).

2. Iraqi wartime personnel losses include 15,000–20,000 killed, 120,000–200,000 deserted, and 86,000 taken prisoner.

3. Iraqi losses during the war included about 500 T-72s—more than half of its pre-war inventory, 200 self-propelled guns—half of its pre-war inventory, and more than half the trucks in the theatre. However, most of Iraq's 2,800 tank transporters—a key strategic mobility asset—survived the war.

4. Of the 300 aircraft lost during the war, 33 were destroyed in combat, 151 were destroyed on the ground, and 115 fled to Iran. Losses by type were as follows:

  • Air-to-air: MiG-29 (5), F-1E (8), MiG-25 (2), MiG-23 (8), MiG-21 (4), Su-7/17 (3), Su-25 (2), Il-76 (1), plus five helicopters.

  • Fled to Iran: Su-24 (24), F-1E (24), MiG-29 (4), Su-22 (40), Su-20 (4), Su-25 (7), MiG-23 (12). These aircraft joined thirty-three civilian transports that fled to Iran before the war.

5. Before the war, Iraq had 594 hardened aircraft shelters; 375 were destroyed or damaged during the war, although many have been repaired since then.

6. Iraq's pre-war navy consisted of about twenty-five major surface combatants: one frigate, thirteen missile patrol boats (seven Osa-I/II, five ex-Kuwaiti TNC-45s, and one ex-Kuwaiti FPB-57), three Polnocny-class amphibious landing ships, nine minelayers, and numerous small boats. Except for an Osa II and a Polnocny that escaped to Iran, all major surface combatants were destroyed or heavily damaged during the war.

7. Iraq may still have a small number of al-Husayn missiles in its inventory. Iraqi accounting of its inventory of SCUD-B missiles and its derivatives as reported to UNSCOM are as follows:

  • Total SCUD-Bs delivered by the Soviet Union: 819; SCUD-Bs launched against Iran: 330; used in training launches: 6; used in experiments and analysis: 55; destroyed unilaterally or by UNSCOM: 11; returned to Soviet Union for testing: 2.

- Total SCUD-Bs modified to al-Husayn: 399; launched against Iran: 189; launched during Gulf War: 88; destroyed unilaterally or by UNSCOM: 122.
- Total SCUD-Bs modified to al-Hijara: ten; launched during Gulf War: five; destroyed unilaterally or by UNSCOM: five.
- Total SCUD-Bs used in al-'Abid experiments: five.

Some of these figures, however, cannot be verified, and scores of al-Husayn missiles may still be hidden in Iraq.

Sources: DoD, *Conduct of the War*, pp. 154, 195-196; *GWAPS*, pp. 9-10, 106-107; House of Representatives, *Intelligence Successes and Failures in Operations Desert Shield/Storm*, pp. 30-32; CIA, *Operation Desert Storm: A Snapshot of the Battlefield*, September 1993; UN Press Release, IK/128, November 5, 1992, pp. 1-2.

APPENDIX II

IRAQ: PRE-WAR GROUND ORDER OF BATTLE

On the eve of the Gulf War, the Iraqi army consisted of ten corps or corps-level formations controlling about sixty-seven divisions, including twelve Republican Guard divisions, six regular armored divisions, three regular mechanized infantry divisions, and forty-six regular infantry divisions. About three-quarters of the army was deployed in the Kuwaiti theatre, with the remainder deployed along the borders with Iran, Turkey, Syria, and within the country to maintain internal security.

Republican Guard Forces Command (2 AD, 3 MD, 7 ID)	Armored/Mechanized Divisions (6 AD, 3 MD)			Infantry Divisions (46 ID)		
Hammurabi Forces (AD)	3d AD	1st MD		2d ID	26th ID	42d ID
Al-Madina al-Munawara Forces (AD)	6th AD	5th MD		4th ID	27th ID	44th ID
Tawakalna 'Ala Allah Forces (MD)	10th AD	51st MD		7th ID	28th ID	45th ID
Baghdad Forces (MD)	12th AD			8th ID	29th ID	46th ID
Al-'Abid Forces (MD)	17th AD			11th ID	30th ID	47th ID
Al-Faw Forces (ID)	52d AD			14th ID	31st ID	48th ID
Nebuchadnezzar Forces (ID)				15th ID	32d ID	49th ID
'Adnan Forces (ID)				16th ID	33d ID	50th ID
Al-Mustafa Forces (ID)				18th ID	34th ID	53d ID
Al-Nida' Forces (ID)				19th ID	35th ID	54th ID
Al-Quds Forces (ID)				20th ID	36th ID	55th ID
Special Forces Division				21st ID	37th ID	56th ID
				22d ID	38th ID	57th ID
Independent Brigades (10-11 Ind Bdes)				23d ID	39th ID	Marsh Forces Command
U/I Independent Armored Brigades (5-6)				24th ID	40th ID	
65th, 66th, 68th Special Forces Brigades				25th ID	41st ID	
440th, 441st Marine Brigades						

Notes:
1. The Al-'Abid, al-Mustafa, al-Nida', and al-Quds Republican Guard divisions were formed after the invasion of Kuwait and remained in Iraq fulfilling internal security functions during the Gulf War.

2. Boldface indicates units located in the Kuwaiti theatre during the Gulf War.

IRAQ: CURRENT GROUND ORDER OF BATTLE

The Iraqi army currently consists of six corps, controlling about thirty divisions, including seven Republican Guard divisions, four regular armored divisions, three regular mechanized divisions, and about fifteen regular infantry divisions. These are deployed as follows: three corps with more than 100,000 troops and sixteen divisions (two Republican Guard divisions, two armored divisions, one mechanized division, and eleven infantry divisions) are deployed facing the Kurdish enclave in the north; about four divisions (including the Special Republican Guard division and elements of several Republican Guard divisions) are deployed in and around Baghdad and elsewhere in the center of the country; and two corps with about 70,000 troops organized into eight divisions (one Republican Guard division, two armored divisions, two mechanized divisions, and three infantry divisions) are located in the south.

Republican Guard (3 AD, 2 MD, 2 ID)

Hammurabi Forces (AD)

Al-Madina al-Munawara Forces (AD)

Al-Nida' Forces (AD)

Al-'Abid Forces (MD)

Baghdad Forces (MD)

Al-Faw Forces (ID)

'Adnan Forces (ID)

Infantry Divisions (15 ID)

2d ID (*Khalid bin al-Walid Forces*)	11th ID (*al-Miqdad Forces*)
4th ID (*al-Qa'qa' Forces*)	14th ID
7th ID (*al-Mansur Forces*)	15th ID (*al-Faruq Forces*)
8th ID (*al-Muthanna Forces*)	16th ID (*Dhu al-Fiqar Forces*)

Armored/Mech Divisions (4 AD, 3 MD)

3d AD (*Salah al-Din Forces*)	1st MD
6th AD	5th MD (*Muhammad al-Qasim Forces*)
10th AD (*al-Nasr Forces*)	51st MD (*Sari al-Jabal Forces*)
52d AD	

18th ID	37th ID (*Ajnadin Forces*)
20th ID	38th ID (*'Umar bin 'Abd al-'Aziz Forces*)
28th ID	57th ID
34th ID (*al-Haritha Forces*)	

Notes:
1. In addition to the divisions listed here, the Iraqi army has a number of independent armor, infantry, artillery, special forces and commando brigades and battalions.

2. Unconfirmed opposition reports also claim that the 22d, 25th, and 42d infantry divisions remain active; these are units which the regime claims to have disbanded after the war.

APPENDIX III

THE IRAQI HIGH COMMAND: 1993[1]

POSITION	NAME
Commander in Chief	Field Marshal Saddam Hussein
Deputy Commander in Chief	Gen. 'Izzat Ibrahim al-Duri[2]
Defense Minister	Gen. 'Ali Hasan al-Majid[3]
Chief of Staff	Lt. Gen. Iyad Futayyih Khalifah al-Rawi[4]
Assistant CoS for Operations	Lt. Gen. Sultan Hashim Ahmad[5]
Assistant CoS for Administration	Lt. Gen. Ahmad Ibrahim Hammash[6]
Assistant CoS for Supplies	Lt. Gen. Iyad Khalil Zaki[7]
Chief of Military Intelligence	Maj. Gen. Fanar Zibin Hasan al-Tikriti[8]
Chief of MoD Political Guidance	Gen. Jabbar Rajab Haddushi[9]
Commander Air & Air Defense Forces	Gen. Muzahim Sa'b Hasan al-Tikriti[10]
Commander of the Republican Guard	Lt. Gen. Ibrahim 'Abd al-Sattar Muhammad[11]
Commander I Corps	Maj. Gen. Mahmud Fayzi Muhammad al-Hazza'[12]
Commander II Corps	Unknown
Commander III Corps	Maj. Gen. Salah Ibrahim
Commander IV Corps	Maj. Gen. 'Abd al-Wahid Shinan al-Ribat[13]
Commander V Corps	Maj. Gen. Nasir Sa'id Tawfiq[14]
Commander Naval and Coastal Defense Forces	Brig. Gen. Khalid Bakr Khadr

Sources: Ofra Bengio, "Iraq," *Middle East Contemporary Survey* (N.Y.: Holmes & Meier), 1986, pp. 391-392; 1987, p. 455; 1988 p. 537; 1990, p. 420; Amatzia Baram and Ofra Bengio, personal correspondence; and *FBIS-NES,* various dates.

Notes:

1. Nearly every general staff officer and corps commander who served during the Gulf War in 1991 had been replaced or reassigned by 1993. General staff officers and corps commanders are generally rotated every twelve to eighteen months, sometimes even more frequently, to prevent any one individual from building a following in the military.

2. Senior civilian party apparatchik who was made a general and appointed to his current position after the Gulf War.

3. Paternal cousin of Saddam who succeeded Lt. Gen. Husayn Kamil al-Majid, another paternal cousin and son-in-law of Saddam.

4. Commander of the Republican Guard during the Gulf War. Succeeded Husayn Rashid Muhammad al-Tikriti, an Arabized Kurd. Most general staff officers and corps commanders are Sunni Arabs, although there are a number of Shi'i Arabs and a few Kurds and Turcomans in the upper ranks of the military.

5. Commanded I and IV Corps during the Iran-Iraq War.

6. Commanded the Republican Guard's al-Madina al-Munawara Forces during the Iran-Iraq War and VII Corps during the Gulf War.

7. Commanded IV Corps and V Corps during the Iran-Iraq War, and IV Corps during the Gulf War.

8. Commanded Special Security during the Kurdish and Shi'i uprising. The latest in a series of commanders of military intelligence since the Gulf War, succeeding Maj. Gen. 'Abd al-Qadr Salman Khamis—a relative of Saddam's from Tikrit, Maj. Gen. Wafiq Jasim Sammara'i, and Maj. Gen. Sabir 'Abd al-'Aziz Husayn al-Duri—who commanded military intelligence during the Gulf War.

9. Succeeded Maj. Gen. Mundhir 'Abd-al-Rahman who was sacked in November 1991, reportedly due to his failure to correct the morale problem in the Iraqi military after the war.

10. Incorrectly reported in the press to have been executed in January 1991.

11. Commanded the 10th Republican Guard Armored Brigade and the Republican Guard's Hammurabi Forces during the Iran-Iraq War. A disproportionate number of senior staff officers and corps commanders formerly served in the Republican Guard, indicating the critical role this organization plays in the military, and in the selection, professional development, and advancement of future senior officers.

12. Served as an alternate commander of the 1st Mechanized Division and the commander of the 5th Mechanized Division during the Iran-Iraq War, and commanded the Jihad Operations Command during the Gulf War.

13. Commanded the 11th Infantry Division and the Republican Guard's Baghdad Forces during the Iran-Iraq War, and VI Corps during the Gulf War.

14. Chief of Staff, VII Corps, during the Gulf War.

APPENDIX IV

IRAQ'S MILITARY-INDUSTRIAL RECONSTRUCTION: AN ASSESSMENT

The dearth of accurate and detailed data concerning the damage done to Iraq's military-industrial infrastructure during the Gulf War and the subsequent reconstruction effort makes it difficult to assess Iraq's current military-industrial capacity. While official Iraqi announcements and foreign press reports have tended to emphasize Iraqi achievements (which are impressive),[1] they have generally overlooked the difficulties faced by the industrial sector in restoring even modest levels of production. A more balanced assessment of Iraq's post-war reconstruction effort can, however, be gleaned from the reports of UNSCOM and IAEA weapons inspectors who have visited Iraq since the war. These reports show that while many military-industrial facilities have been rebuilt, few are functioning at more than a fraction of their pre-war capacity.

Iraq's success in rapidly rebuilding its military-industrial infrastructure can be attributed to the fact that before the bombing began the regime ordered that critical equipment be removed from facilities and dispersed in nearby villages and fields. After the war, equipment that was not removed was salvaged from the wreckage of bombed out buildings, repaired, and returned to service. Non-critical civilian industries may have also been stripped of machinery and fixtures in order to repair key military industrial plants. The Iraqis have even stripped salvageable components from dual-use machinery that had been disabled under the supervision of UN inspectors.

The case of the al-Rabiya mechanical workshop provides a particularly outstanding example of what the Iraqis can accomplish when they apply sufficient manpower and resources. The al-Rabiya workshop was largely destroyed by a U.S. cruise missile strike on January 17, 1993. Because of the publicity surrounding the operation, the Iraqis attached particular importance to the reconstruction of this site as a symbol of Iraqi defiance and determination. The al-Rabiya workshop was rebuilt in six weeks in a massive round-the-clock effort. According to IAEA inspectors who visited the site just ten days after the attack:

> The Iraqi side is cleaning up and rebuilding the site with determination to put it back in business within a few months. Thousands of people and hundreds of pieces of heavy equipment are committed on an around the clock basis. Large flood lights were in evidence throughout the facility. A large open field just to the west of the plant was rapidly being filled with rubble. The Iraqi side is literally removing rubble from one side of a building while they are re-building walls on the other side.[2]

---

[1] For instance, Iraqi government officials claimed in January 1992 that Iraq had restored 85 percent of its pre-war oil refining capacity and 75 percent of its pre-war electrical power grid, and had repaired nearly every bridge destroyed during the war. *WT*, January 12, 1992, p. 14.

[2] IAEA-17, S/25411, March 13, 1993, p. 7.

Another IAEA inspection team visited the site in early May 1993 and reported that:

> Today, the facility has been turned into a showcase—all destroyed buildings [have been rebuilt and] are nicely finished inside and out, the new administration building is occupied, the whole area is landscaped, monuments (including recovered scraps from cruise missiles) have been erected, and an exhibition center that documents the whole reconstruction is a required stop for all visitors. Most of the machine tools and equipment were reinstalled in the workshop buildings [and] many of the machine tools have been repaired.[1]

Because rebuilding al-Rabiya was a priority effort due to its symbolic value to the regime, it almost certainly does not accurately reflect the status of the broader reconstruction effort, and it would be incorrect to draw general conclusions from this one case.

An interesting counterpoint to this example is the case of the al-Kindi (SAAD-16) missile research and development complex near Mosul. Before the war, this facility was touted as the main missile research and development center in the country.[2] In fact, it has recently become clear that the facility had never been completed because Iraq was unable to acquire vital missile research and development and production technology following the establishment of the Missile Technology Control Regime in 1987 and the concomitant adoption of increasingly stringent export rules by key supplier states. The al-Kindi facility was destroyed during the war and since then has been rebuilt as a rocket propellant research and development facility. However, it is not considered operational and its potential contribution to Iraq's current missile research and development effort has been assessed as quite limited.[3] This case illustrates the point that the fact that a facility has been rebuilt does not necessarily mean that it is adequately staffed with trained personnel, supplied with sufficient raw materials, and equipped with serviceable equipment needed to sustain a significant research, development, or production effort.

Regarding the condition of Iraq's inventory of machine tools—a crucial factor in its efforts to restore its military-industrial infrastructure—IAEA inspectors have offered the general observation that the performance of many machine tools in Iraq has been "degraded by war damage, multiple movements [to prevent] further war damage and poor work conditions and maintenance." However, they note that the performance of individual machines "can be

---

[1] IAEA-19, S/25982, June 21, 1993, pp. 13-14. Another report noted however that some machines at al-Rabiya had not been repaired due to a lack of spares. IAEA-18, S/25666, April 26, 1993, p. 15.

[2] One pre-war account of the site described it, in the words of a British engineer who had visited it, as "absolutely brilliant," an "ideal facility," without peer anywhere in Europe. *Der Spiegel*, February 4, 1991, pp. 33-35, in *JPRS-TND*, February 25, 1991, p. 44. See also: *The Middle East*, June 1989, p. 21; *MidEast Markets*, May 1, 1989, p. 12.

[3] IAEA-18, April 26, 1993, p. 7.

improved through refurbishment and compensations for systematic errors."[1] Thus, many of the functioning machine tools in Iraq could be used to produce precision components and fittings for advanced weapons only with great difficulty.

Perhaps the most revealing comments regarding the current status of Iraq's industrial infrastructure were made by Minister of Labor 'Umid Midhat Mubarak in a recent interview in which he stated that thousands of factories have been closed down and many are operating at far below capacity due to a shortage of raw materials and spares. According to Mubarak, the "devastating effects of the war," as well as "the scarcity of raw materials and spare parts resulting from the international sanctions" has "forced the closure of the bulk of Iraqi public sector and private sector industries." As a result, "for the first time in Iraq's history, we are suffering from rampant unemployment as a result of the sanctions." He added that Iraq was having great difficulty in rebuilding many sites destroyed during the war due to a lack of equipment and spares.[2]

Thus, the weight of the evidence available from all sources indicates that while much of Iraq's military-industrial infrastructure has been rebuilt since the war, it is operating at only a fraction of its pre-war capacity due to the lingering effects of the war, a shortage of raw materials, the poor condition of functioning machinery, and an inability to repair broken machinery as a result of a lack of spare parts.[3]

As a final comment, it is worth noting that the rapid recovery of Iraq's military industries is rather unexceptional, when seen in historical context. For instance, a study conducted by the U.S. Strategic Bombing Survey after World War II concerning the effect of Allied bombing on Germany's ball bearing industry noted that "it proved more difficult to put [ball bearing] plants out of operation than had been foreseen." The report went on to say that "even direct hits on vital processes did not put a plant out of operation" since "general purpose machinery" in one part of the factory was often "quickly adapted for use in another" to help restore production capacity, while "most of the stocks of raw materials and semifinished bearings were not harmed beyond salvage."[4] Similarly, in its study of the attacks on the German oil industry, the survey noted that "plants that had been knocked out completely were brought back into production in relatively few weeks." This "very rapid rate of recuperation" was "in part accomplished by cannibalizing equipment from badly bombed plants and from new plants under construction to keep other plants going and also in part resulted from taking manpower and materials from other industries of lesser importance."[5]

---

[1] IAEA-19, June 21, 1993, p. 7.

[2] *Jordan Times*, April 10, 1993, p. 2. Likewise, Minister of Industry 'Amir Hammudi al-Sa'di said in a recent interview that while about 90 percent of the industrial capacity damaged during the Gulf War has been repaired, most factories are operating at between 10 to 50 percent of capacity due to a lack of raw materials and access to export markets. *NYT*, July 21, 1993, p. 6.

[3] Gates, "Statement of the Director of Central Intelligence," March 27, 1992, p. 8.

[4] USSBS, Overall Report (European War), September 30, 1945, p. 29.

[5] *Ibid.*, p. 42.

The survey's study of Germany's aviation industry concluded that "machine tools and heavy manufacturing equipment of all kinds are very difficult to destroy or to damage beyond repair by bombing attacks. Buildings housing such equipment may be burned down and destroyed but, after clearing away the wreckage, it has been found, more often than not, that heavy equipment, when buried under tons of debris may be salvaged and put back into operation in a relatively short time and with comparatively little difficulty."[1] Recent experience in Iraq thus simply repeats the experience of nearly half a century ago; its ability to rapidly rebuild its military-industrial infrastructure should not have come as such a surprise.

---

[1] USSBS, Aircraft Division Industry Report, November 2, 1945, p. 8.

IRAQ'S MILITARY-INDUSTRIAL INFRASTRUCTURE*

Location	Facility	Activities	Status
Nuclear Related Facilities			
Abu Sukhayr	Carbonate ore mine	Extraction of uranium from carbonate ores (exploratory)	Non-functioning
Akashat	Phosphate mine	Extraction of uranium from phosphate ores	Functioning
Baghdad	Iraqi Atomic Energy Commission	Headquarters of civilian and military nuclear programs	Unknown
Baghdad	PC3 Project Headquarters	Oversaw and coordinated weaponization effort	Unknown
Baghdad	National Computer Center	Computer support for weaponization effort	Functioning
Baghdad	Rashdiya Engineering Design Center	Engineering support for centrifuge design work	Functioning
Baghdad	Geological and Survey Institute	Advise concerning uranium mining and recovery processes	Functioning
Batra	Al-Amin ('Uqba bin Nafi') machine shops**	Calutron components	Functioning
Batra	Al-Radwan ('Uqba bin Nafi') machine shops	Calutron components	Functioning
Daura	SEHEE works	Calutron and centrifuge components	Functioning
Dur	Salah al-Din (SAAD 13) electronics complex	Calutron components	Heavily damaged, rebuilt, partly functioning
Falluja	Al-Amir ('Uqba bin Nafi') machine shops	Calutron components	Functioning
Falluja	Saddam machine shops	Centrifuge components	Functioning
Al-Hatra	Al-Hatra explosives test range	Weaponization work	Functioning
Iskandariya	Al-Qa'qa' explosives plant and test range	Weaponization work	Heavily damaged, rebuilt, partly functioning
Mosul	Al-Jazira feedstock plant	Calutron and centrifuge feedstock production	Non-functioning

Location	Facility	Activities	Status
Musayib	Al-Athir Materials Research Center	Primary nuclear weapons research, development, and design (weaponization) center	Destroyed
Musayib	Hittin explosives test range	Weaponization work	Functioning
Nasiriya	Ur Aluminum Factory	Centrifuge components	Functioning
Al-Qa'im	Uranium ore processing plant	Yellow cake production	Destroyed
Sharqat	Sharqat calutron enrichment plant	Calutron enrichment facility	Destroyed
Taji	Nasr machine shops	Centrifuge components	Functioning
Tarmiya	Tarmiya calutron enrichment plant	Calutron enrichment facility	Destroyed
Tuwaitha	Tuwaitha Nuclear Research Center	Primary nuclear research and development center. Site of Tammuz I and II, and IRT-5000 research reactors, and laboratories researching uranium enrichment and reprocessing technologies	Destroyed
Al-Walid	Badr engineering shops	Centrifuge components	Unknown
Al-Walid	Al-Furat gas centrifuge production facility	Primary centrifuge production facility and possible intended site for centrifuge enrichment plant	Destroyed
Za'faraniya	Al-Rabiya (al-Nida') machine shops	Calutron components	Heavily damaged, rebuilt, partly functioning
Za'faraniya	Dijla (al-Zaura) electronics complex	Calutron components	Functioning

CBW Related Facilities***

Location	Facility	Activities	Status
Falluja	Falluja CW precursor plant	Nerve agent precursors	Destroyed
Musayib	Al-Hakam probable BW production facility	BW production (planned)	Engaged in animal feed production
Salman Pak	Salman Pak BW production facility	BW research, development, production, and storage	Destroyed
Samarra	Muthanna CW Production facility	CW research, development, production, and storage	Destroyed

Location	Facility	Activities	Status
Ballistic Missile and Supergun Related Facilities			
Baghdad	Ibn al-Haytham missile research and development center	Missile research and development (established after the Gulf War)	Functioning
Daura	Daura missile launcher workshop (Project 144)	Al-Walid and al-Nida' mobile missile launchers	Destroyed
Falluja	Dhu al-Fiqar missile factory (Project 395)	Badr 2000 motor cases and nozzles	Damaged, rebuilt, partly functioning
Iskandariya	Al-Qa'qa' explosives plant and test range	Al-Husayn missile warhead modification and filling, al-'Abid missile stage separation work, supergun propellant storage	Damaged, rebuilt, partly functioning
Iskandariya	Unidentified	Supergun component storage	Unknown
Jabal Hamrin	Supergun (350 mm) site	Supergun prototype testing	Destroyed
Jabal Sinjar	Supergun (350 mm) site	Proposed site of second supergun	Unfinished
Karbala	Al-Anbar Space Research Center	Al-'Abid missile test range	Unknown
Latifiya	Taj al-Ma'arik (Bilat al-Shuhada) missile factory (Project 395)	Badr 2000 solid fuel mixing and casting	Damaged, rebuilt, partly functioning
Mosul	Al-Kindi (SAAD 16) missile research and development center	Missile research and development (unfinished)	Damaged, rebuilt, non-functioning
Musayib	Al-Yawm al-'Azim missile factory (Project 395)	Badr 2000 motor assembly and testing	Damaged, rebuilt, partly functioning
Musayib	Hittin explosives test range	Supergun propellant testing	Functioning
Taji	Nasr missile factory (Project 144)	Modification of SCUD-B, HY-2, and SA-2 missiles; missile maintenance, repair, and storage activities	Destroyed
Tal 'Afar	Tal 'Afar missile test range	Test range for al-Hussayn and al-'Abbas missiles	Unknown
Al-Rafah	Shahiyat missile test facility (Project 1728)	Liquid fuel rocket motor (SCUD B, HY-2, SA-2) engineering and testing	Damaged, rebuilt, partly functioning
Western Zone	Fixed missile launchers	28 launchers operational with 28 more planned or under construction	Destroyed

Location	Facility	Activities	Status

Conventional Arms Production and Maintenance Facilities†

Location	Facility	Activities	Status
Baghdad	Ministry of Industry and Military Industrialization (MIMI) building	MIMI headquarters-oversaw military-industrial effort	Heavily damaged, rebuilt, functioning
Baghdad	Nahrawan (SAAD 38) munitions plant	Cardoen FAE and CBU bombs, shell casings, and fuzes	Heavily damaged, rebuilt, partly functioning
Baghdad	Mansur military electronics complex	Unknown	Unknown
Basra	Sawari boat factory	Armed patrol boats	Unknown
Dur	Salah al-Din (SAAD 13) military electronics complex	Thomspon CSF Tiger G and Rasit radars, Jaguar tactical radios, battlefield computers, and electronic components (licensed production)	Heavily damaged, rebuilt
Falluja	Saddam (SAAD 5) Ordnance Factory	Artillery (D-30 and Ababil), ammunition, and optical sights	Unknown
Falluja	Muthanna munitions plant	Naval mines and explosives	Unknown
Al-Hatra	Al-Hatra explosives test range	Explosives (FAE and CBU) testing	Functioning
Iskandariya	Al-Qa'qa' explosives plant and test range	Bombs, explosives, and rocket propellant production and testing	Heavily damaged, rebuilt, partly functioning
Mahawil	Nasr munitions plant	Bombs and rocket artillery	Unknown
Mosul	Mosul (SAAD 21) munitions plant	Ammunition	Unknown
Mosul	Mosul (SAAD 24) CBW protective gear plant	Gas masks and CBW protective gear	Functioning
Musayib	Hittin explosives plant	Explosives, propellants, ammunition, and fuzes	Functioning
Musayib	Al-Furnas helicopter maintenance and design center	Unknown	Functioning (established after the Gulf War)
Salman Pak	Military electronics complex	Unknown	Functioning
Samawa	Samawa armored vehicle maintenance facility	Armored vehicle maintenance, repair, and refits	Unknown
Taji	Nasr armored vehicle assembly and maintenance facility	Tank and armored vehicle assembly, maintenance, repair, and refits	Heavily damaged

Location	Facility	Activities	Status
Taji	Nasr aircraft engine maintenance facility	Aircraft engine maintenance, repair, and testing	Heavily damaged
Taji	Nasr ordnance plant	Artillery and ammunition	Heavily damaged, rebuilt, partly functioning
Al-Walid	Qadisiya ordnance plant	Small guns and anti-aircraft artillery production and maintenance	Unknown
Yusufiya	Al-Amin ('Uqba bin Nafi') machine shops	T-72 maintenance and spares	Non-functioning
Yusufiya	Badr munitions plant	Bombs and ammunition	Unknown
Za'faraniya	Dijla (Al-Zaura) electronics complex	Computer hardware and software	Functioning

SOURCE: Various IAEA inspection reports; Timmerman, "Iraq Rebuilds its Military Industries," June 29, 1993; MEDNEWS Special Report: Iraqi Arms Production, May 8, 1989; and 37th FW, "Nighthawks Over Iraq," 1991.

* This table consists largely of facilities active before the Gulf War. Facilities which remain active are no longer engaged in proscribed activities; many, however, are subject to UNSCOM monitoring.

** Badr, Bilat al-Shuhada, Hittin, al-Kindi, Muthanna, Nasr, al-Nida', Qadisiya, al-Qa'qa', Saddam, Salah al-Din, SEHEE, 'Uqba bin Nafi', and al-Zaura are the names of various state industrial establishments involved in weapons production.

*** In addition, over twenty CBW storage facilities (including refrigerated bunkers believed to be for BW storage) were located at air bases and other sites throughout the country.

† State establishments involved in conventional arms production which have not been located and are thus not listed in the table include: Anfal (artillery rockets); Faris (bombs, explosives); al-Jalil (mortars); al-Mu'tasim (observation towers, rocket launchers); al-Nasira (RPG-7s); al-Qadisiya (sniper rifles, optical sights); al-Quds, Tabuq and Yarmuk (assault rifles, small arms ammunition); and Tariq (pistols).

APPENDIX V

A NOTE ON IRAQI MILITARY APPELLATIONS

As part of President Saddam Hussein's drive to establish Iraq as a regional superpower, the regime has pursued a conscious cultural-ideological policy involving the manipulation of highly evocative symbols and themes from the country's Arab-Islamic and ancient Mesopotamian past, in order to mobilize the population in support of this effort.[1] Accordingly, many military units, military-industrial establishments, and weapons are named after historical battles, military heroes, and famous personalities from the past. The following is a short glossary of some of the most frequently used names and their significance:

al-'Abbas: al-'Abbas bin 'Abd al-Muttalib, uncle and brother-in-law of the Prophet Muhammad (d. 652 C.E.). Early Muslim convert and eponymous ancestor of the 'Abbasid caliphs. Also the name of a locally-produced missile.

'Adnan: Saddam's late cousin and brother-in-law, Defense Minister Gen. 'Adnan Khayrallah Talfah (d. 1989 C.E.). Also a Republican Guard division and a locally-produced airborne early warning aircraft.

Ajnadin: battle in which the Muslim forces defeated the Byzantines in 634 C.E., setting the stage for the conquest of Palestine. Also an honorific used by the 37th Infantry Division.

al-Anfal: "the spoils" in Arabic. The name of a *sura* (chapter) in the Qur'an. Also the name of a state establishment involved in the production of artillery rockets, and a series of brutal military campaigns against Kurdish and Shi'i insurgents and civilians in the late 1980s.

al-Athir: 'Izz al-Din bin al-Athir, medieval Arab chronicler (d. 1233 C.E.). Also the name of Iraq's principal nuclear weapon research, development, and design center.

Badr: battle in which the Prophet Muhammad and his early followers won their first major victory, defeating the Meccans in 624 C.E.. Also the name of a state industrial establishment involved in the production of arms and a planned locally-produced missile.

Dhu al-Fiqar: famous two pointed sword that the Prophet Muhammad acquired as booty during the battle of Badr. Also the name of a ballistic missile production facility and an honorific used by the 16th Infantry Division.

al-Hakam: Umayyad caliph in Muslim Spain and patron of the arts and sciences (d. 976 C.E.). Also the name of a planned biological warfare production facility.

---

[1] Amatzia Baram, *Culture, History & Ideology in the Formation of Ba'thist Iraq, 1968-89* (New York: St. Martin's Press, 1991).

Hammurabi: ancient Babylonian king, empire-builder, and lawgiver (d. 1750 B.C.E.). Also the name of a Republican Guard armored division.

Ibn al-Haytham: noted medieval Arab astronomer, mathematician, and lens maker (d. 1039 C.E.). Also the name of Iraq's principal post-war missile research and development facility.

al-Hijara: "the stones" in Arabic. From a verse in the Qur'an and an oblique reference to the Palestinian uprising against Israel. Also the name of a locally-produced missile.

Hittin: epic battle in which the great Islamic military hero Salah al-Din decisively defeated the Crusaders in 1187 C.E., leading to the reconquest of Jerusalem. Also an honorific used by the IVth Army Corps.

al-Husayn: al-Husayn bin 'Ali, grandson of the Prophet Muhammad and the third Shi'i Imam (d. 680 C.E.). Massacred by Umayyad forces at Karbala, and revered by Shi'i Muslims. Also the name of a locally-produced missile.

Khalid bin al-Walid: one of the great Arab generals (d. 642 C.E.). Served under the Prophet Muhammad and his successor, Abu Bakr. Led Muslim forces in the conquest of Syria and Iraq. Also an honorific used by the 2d Infantry Division.

al-Kindi: famous medieval Arab thinker with contributions in astronomy, medicine, engineering, and music (d. 873 C.E.). Also the name of a ballistic missile research and development facility near Mosul.

Mansur: 'Abbasid caliph who move the capital of the empire to Baghdad, providing the impetus to its emergence as a great city (d. 775 C.E.). Also the name of a state establishment producing military electronics and an honorific used by the 7th Infantry Division.

Mu'tasim: 'Abbasid caliph (d. 842 C.E.). Also the name of a state establishment involved in the production of military equipment.

Muthanna: Muthanna bin Haritha, Arab tribal chief, military leader, and early Muslim convert (d. 637 C.E.). Hero of the Islamic conquest of Iraq and the battle of Qadisiya. Also the name of a state establishment involved in the production of chemical weapons, and an honorific used by the 8th Infantry Division.

Nasr: "victory" in Arabic. Also the name of a state establishment involved in the production of arms and an honorific used by the 10th Armored Division.

Nebuchadnezzar: ancient Babylonian king (d. 562 B.C.E.). Babylon reached the zenith of its power under his rule. Also the name of a Republican Guard infantry division.

al-Nida': "the call" in Arabic. Term with both religious and nationalistic connotations. The name of a state industrial establishment involved in the production of arms, a Republican Guard armored division, a locally-produced mobile missile launcher, and the code name for the invasion of Kuwait.

Qadisiya: epic battle in which the Muslims decisively defeated the Persians in 637 C.E. near Hilla, setting the stage for the conquest of Iraq. Also the name of a state establishment involved in the production of arms and an honorific used by the IIId Army Corps.

al-Qa'qa': Al-Qa'qa' bin 'Amr al-Tamimi, poet and celebrated hero of the battles of Yarmuk and Qadisiya (d. 660 C.E.). Also the name of a state establishment involved in the production of explosives and an honorific used by the 4th Infantry Division.

Sa'd: Sa'd bin Abi-Waqqas, one of the great Arab generals (d. 670 C.E.). Led Muslim forces in their route of the Persians at Qadisiya. Also the name of a state establishment that served as the prime contractor for numerous military-industrial projects (i.e. SAAD 16, SAAD 24, etc.).

Salah al-Din: great Islamic military leader and empire builder (d. 1193 C.E.). Led Islamic forces to victory over the Crusaders in the Battle of Hittin and the reconquest of Jerusalem. Also the name of a state establishment involved in the production of military electronics and an honorific used by the 3d Mechanized Division.

Sawari: reference to the naval battle of Dhat al-Sawari off the coast of modern Turkey in which the Muslims defeated the Byzantines in 655 C.E.. Also the name of a state establishment that produces small patrol boats.

Tawakalna 'Ala Allah: "in God we trust" in Arabic. Popular religious invocation derived from a Qur'anic verse. Also the name of a Republican Guard mechanized division and a key military campaign during the Iran-Iraq War.

'Uqba bin Nafi': one of the great Arab generals who led the Muslim conquests of North Africa (d. 683 C.E.). Also the name of a state establishment involved in the production military and civilian products.

al-Walid: Umayyad caliph (d. 715 C.E.). The Umayyad empire reached its zenith under his rule. Also the name of a locally-produced mobile missile launcher.

Yarmuk: battle in which the Muslims defeated the Byzantines near the Sea of Galilee in 636 C.E., paving the way for the conquest of Syria. Also an honorific used by the IId Army Corps.

RECENT PUBLICATIONS OF THE WASHINGTON INSTITUTE

For a complete listing or to order publications, write or call The Washington Institute for Near East Policy, 1828 L Street, NW, Suite 1050, Washington, D.C. 20036 Phone (202) 452-0650, Fax (202) 223-5364